LEGAL KALEIDOSCOPE: AN ANTHOLOGY OF LEGAL PERSPECTIVES

LEGAL KALEIDOSCOPE: AN ANTHOLOGY OF LEGAL PERSPECTIVES

Jaykumar Bhongale

ELIVA PRESS

ISBN: 978-99949-8-774-0

Cover Design: Eliva Press
Cover Image: Ingimage
Email: info@elivapress.com
Website: www.elivapress.com

This Eliva Press imprint is published by the registered company Eliva Press Global Ltd. part of Eliva Press S.R.L. Publishing Group

The registered company address is: Pope Hennessy Street Level 2, Hennessy Tower Port Louis, Mauritius
Eliva Press S.R.L. Publishing Group address is: Bulevardul Moscova 21, Chisinau, Moldova, Europe

LEGAL KALEIDOSCOPE: AN ANTHOLOGY OF LEGAL PERSPECTIVE

DR. JAYKUMAR BHONGALE

Edited by:
Mr. Oishik Bhattachrya & Ms. Saheli Chakraborty

TABLE OF CONTENTS

Courts and their Interpretation of 'Cruelty' under section 498-A of the Indian Penal Code: A Critique

DR. JAYKUMAR BHONGALE*

MR. OISHIK BHATTACHARYA**

Abstract

In recent years, section 498-A has been severely criticised for being a redundant provision of the Indian Penal Code, frequently abused by women to harass their husbands. The Law Commission of India, in its 243rd Report questioned the relevance of this section on the ground that the number of acquittals in cases of matrimonial cruelty is extremely high while convictions are abysmally low. At the same time, research suggests that violence against women in their matrimonial homes is not just common but has fairly increased in current times, on account of Covid-19. As Courts contribute significantly to the flawed perception of section 498-A, it is necessary to understand the manner in which the provision has been interpreted by them. This paper attempts to study selected decisions of the Supreme Court and various High Courts of India in order to trace the contours of matrimonial 'cruelty' in the Indian Penal Code. The author argues that the high rate of acquittals is the fallout of interpretational errors in decision-making and does not necessarily point towards the dishonesty of the victim, no matter how incredulous the courts and judges may find her to be.

The Context:

In April, 2020, the United Nations [hereinafter, "UN"] drew global attention to the growing violence against women in the midst of the Covid-19 pandemic.[1] Research revealed that with rising number of infections across States and the unavoidable imposition of containment and lockdown measures to protect people, several women

---

* Assistant Professor & Research Coordinator at Bharati Vidyapeeth Deemed to be University, New Law College Pune.

**Student of BBA LLB SEM VII, Bharati Vidyapeeth Deemed to be University, New Law College Pune.

[1] *The Shadow Pandemic: Violence against women during Covid 19*, UN WOMEN (Feb. 25, 2021), https://www.unwomen.org/en/news/in-focus/in-focus-gender-equality-in-covid-19-response/violence-against-women-during-covid-19.

were trapped with their abusive partners inside homes.[2] A rise in the number of calls to helplines and shelter homes for protection from violence against such partners became a matter of concern in countries all over the world. In fact, UN Women called this phenomenon a 'shadow pandemic' of violence against women, festering amidst Covid-19.[3]

In India, like in the rest of the world, the problem of marriage-based violence was found to have increased during the pandemic. Such incidents led a number of Indian Courts to take *suo motu* cognizance of such cases and issue measures and directions to prevent their occurrence.[4] However, the problem continues to rise, making it essential to revisit and re-examine section 498-A of the Indian Penal Code [hereinafter, "IPC"].

Section 498-A was originally codified to protect women from violence inside their matrimonial homes. However, in recent years, it has been cornered by lawyers, judges, police and the public on grounds of abuse and redundancy. The provision lost a major chunk of its appeal and efficacy in 2017, when the Supreme Court [hereinafter, "SC"] passed an important judgment in an inexplicably hurried manner, with a misplaced need to silence women trapped in violent marriages.[5] This decision of the SC was based on an understanding from its pre-existing jurisprudence that section 498-A of the IPC is grossly abused by Indian women to "unleash legal terrorism" on innocent husbands.[6]

This judgment was perhaps the most insensitive in a series of unsympathetic decisions of the SC in such cases, since it reduced the nuanced concept of family-based violence captured in section 498-A to an ordinary civil dispute. Instead, it called for the constitution of 'Family Welfare Committees' to look into the veracity of a complaint of

---

[2] Phumzile Mlambo-Ngcuka, *Violence against women and girls: the shadow pandemic*, UN WOMEN (Apr. 6, 2020), https://www.unwomen.org/en/news/stories/2020/4/statement-ed-phumzile-violence-against-women-during-pandemic.

[3] *Id.*

[4] Devika Sharma, *J&K HC: Rising Domestic Violence amid Lockdown- Court suggests measures and directions, takes cognizance suo motu*, THE SCC ONLINE BLOG (Apr. 19, 2020), https://www.scconline.com/blog/post/2020/04/19/jk-hc-rising-domestic-violence-amid-lockdown-court-suggests-measures-and-directions-takes-cognizance-suo-motu/.

[5] Rajesh Sharma v. State of Uttar Pradesh, A.I.R. 2017 S.C. 821 (India).

[6] Sushil Kumar Sharma v. Union of India, A.I.R. 2005 S.C. 3100 (India).

domestic violence before criminal proceedings could be initiated.[7] In September 2018, the SC modified its erroneous ruling in Rajesh Sharma's case and did away with the constitution of Family Welfare Committees. However, it continued to echo sentiments that were captured in its earlier decisions, highlighting the abuse of section 498-A.[8]

Rajesh Sharma's case was preceded by Arnesh Kumar's case,[9] in which the SC laid down a set of guidelines to contain the rigour of section 498-A. Here, the Court's primary focus was to prevent the police from arresting the husband and his relatives in case his wife has filed an FIR under section 498-A. While doing so, the SC pointed out that the provision has been grossly abused by women to harass their husbands when they did not meet their demands.

Even prior to Arnesh Kumar's case, the SC had noted in two other cases that the fact of women abusing section 498-A is well-known.[10] Apart from the Apex Court, the 243rd Law Commission Report, which studied the challenges to section 498-A, reiterated the needlessness of this provision. Quoting judgments of the SC that labelled battered women as "disgruntled wives" and presuming that women abused the section to settle domestic scores with their husbands, the Report stated that a miniscule portion of these cases resulted in convictions while the rest of them ended in acquittals.[11] It also stated that the dismal number of acquittals in section 498-A cases suggests the irrelevance of this section.[12] Recommendations of the Law Commission ranged from revisiting the need to retain section 498-A in the IPC to making the offence compoundable.[13]

---

[7] *Supra* note 5.

[8] *Supreme Court modifies its own 2017 ruling that had ordered constitution of 'family welfare committees' to look into veracity of Section 498A (cruelty/dowry) complaints*, The Leaflet (Sept. 14, 2018), https://www.theleaflet.in/supreme-court-modifies-its-own-2017-ruling-that-had-ordered-constitution-of-family-welfare-committees-to-look-into-veracity-of-section-498a-dowry-complaints/.

[9] Arnesh Kumar v. State of Bihar, (2014) 8 S.C.C. 273 (India).

[10] Preeti Gupta v. State of Jharkhand, (2010) 7 S.C.C. 667 (India).

[11] Law Commission of India, *243rd Report on Section 498A of Indian Penal Code, 1860* (2012).

[12] *Id.*

[13] *Id.*

Ever since the provision has been portrayed as monstrous, especially by the SC, there has been a significant impact on how other actors in the criminal justice mechanism, such as the police, respond to victims of matrimonial cruelty.

A Maze of Evidence and Interpretation:

While it is well established that the number of acquittals under a certain provision cannot by itself point towards its irrelevance, it is also necessary to examine how courts have interpreted matrimonial cruelty under section 498-A and why many of these acquittals may be unjustified.

It is argued that courts have erred in their understanding of the principle of 'beyond reasonable doubt' while appreciating evidence, circumstances and the conduct of victims in section 498-A cases. It is also argued that the web of confusion around section 498-A leads to the creation of insurmountable barriers for victims when they are attempting to access justice while experiencing violent marriages. The incredulity associated with victims approaching the police or courts with criminal complaints of matrimonial cruelty is hazardous as it attempts to further endanger the oppressed, thereby perpetuating an endless cycle of revictimization and injustice by the very institutions that stand to promote the cause of justice.

The SC's approach, formed on the basis of presumptions and unsubstantiated by data or even an indication of the need thereof, deactivates an existing legal provision by misinterpretation. Hence, before further steps are taken by the SC to pin down section 498-A of the IPC, it is important to dissect decision-making in this area.

To this end, the paper approaches the problem of acquittals under section 498-A from two perspectives: *firstly*, it examines how courts err in their application of the principle of 'beyond reasonable doubt' in cases under section 498-A and *secondly*, it studies the inconsistent interpretation of matrimonial cruelty by courts while reeling under the weight of evidentiary standards in matters of violence within the family. In this regard, it is argued that context cannot be ignored when judges decide whether or not acts of violence qualify as matrimonial cruelty within the meaning of this provision. In doing so, selected judgments of the Apex Court as well as High Courts have been examined to locate inconsistencies in the interpretation of section 498-A.

It is argued that many acquittals are the consequence of Courts' erroneous approach in understanding the nuances of violence or their inability to appreciate existing evidence in such serious offences that happen in the privacy of homes. These flaws in method and reasoning compromise the rights of victims and put them in a tight spot by amplifying existing patriarchal biases and prejudices against them. The combined effect of these cases is that judges end up ideating the contours of cruelty even when the law clearly lays down its contents. Errors in judicial approach cannot be reasons to either treat victims of matrimonial cruelty with suspicion or nullify the impact of a protective legal provision by judicial action or the lack thereof.

From the perspective of the victim, in cognizable offences such as section 498-A, errors of judicial approach leading to wrongful acquittals may mean the difference between her life and death (if the victim is alive). Not only that, undeserved acquittals create a culture of impunity and encourage a state policy of tolerance towards violence.[14] These ensure, in turn, that batterers feel encouraged to perpetuate acts of violence against women.[15]

Matrimonial Cruelty as a Penal Offence

While the IPC does not *define* matrimonial cruelty under section 498-A, it does provide an explanation which sets out when wilful conduct may be considered cruel. For cruelty to have occurred, it is sufficient that willful conduct exists which drives a woman to commit suicide or causes grave injury to her life, limb or health.[16] Health refers to both physical as well as mental health under the provision. Apart from this, the second limb of the explanation states that if a woman is harassed by her husband or his relatives, or is coerced by them to meet unlawful demands for property or valuable security, such harassment will also qualify as matrimonial cruelty.[17]

---

[14] Emily J. Sack, *Battered Women and the State, The Struggle for the Future of Domestic Violence Policy*, WIS. LAW REV., 1657 (2004).
[15] *Id.*
[16] The Indian Penal Code, 1860, No. 45, Acts of Parliament, 1860 (India).
[17] *Id.*

In toto, section 498-A provides for two categories of matrimonial cruelty: while the first one encompasses any and every form of violence of a certain *degree* that can qualify as matrimonial cruelty, the second limb identifies harassment of a very purposive and *specific* nature that can be brought within the meaning of section 498-A.

Further, the law makes it abundantly clear that whether or not cruelty was meted out to victims is a question of fact. Thus, how courts appreciate facts in such cases is crucial to the determination of acquittal or conviction.

Courts and their interpretation of 'Cruelty' under section 498-A

Ignoring Omissions

While the criminal act contemplated in section 498-A may be by way of commission as well as omission, Courts have often passed decisions that obfuscate the meaning of matrimonial cruelty. In order to determine whether an act is grave enough to constitute cruelty in a matrimonial relationship, testing the impact of such an act in terms of it causing grave injury to the victim's life, limb or health is sufficient. Moreover, while determining such impact, it is also necessary to keep in mind that the act in question occurs in intimate relationships. Therefore, whether an omission or a commission would be sufficiently grave to constitute cruelty cannot be construed by isolating incidents from the context of the family and family-based relationships. For example, an omission on the part of the husband to take his half-dead wife to the hospital for several hours after she has sustained injuries under suspicious conditions inside their house should clearly constitute cruelty within the meaning of section 498-A, since it is willful conduct that gravely endangers the victim's life and health. However, Courts have held otherwise and in doing so, have acquitted the accused while gravely endangering the rights of women injured or killed by their violent spouses and their families.

In *Arvind Singh v State of Bihar*,[18] the SC overturned the appellant's conviction despite the fact that he had been convicted by the Trial Court and the High Court, stating *inter alia* that the lack of "outside witnesses" made the Prosecution's case less reliable. Interestingly, the two-judge Bench of the SC in this case pointed out that there were

---

[18] Arvind Singh v State of Bihar, (2001) 3 S.C.R. 218 (India).

several lacunae in the investigation of the police, as a consequence of which precious evidence that may have helped the Prosecution's case had probably been lost. Facts on record revealed that Minta Devi, the victim in this case, was burnt to death in the presence of Arvind Singh and his family members, who made no effort whatsoever to save her. Not only that, they did not even make an effort to assuage her pain by taking her to a hospital or calling a doctor, as she lay on the cot with 85 percent burn injuries. The victim's family was also not informed about the incident and they arrived several hours later, only when a neighbor informed the family about Minta's "accident."

In cases such as Arvind Singh's, where violence is veiled by privacy and the victim is generally on her own, such omissions raise significant questions around the innocence of the accused and clearly point towards an element of guilt. However instead of contextualizing facts and comprehending them in the light of family-based violence, the SC, in an effort to add layers to the meaning of cruelty, stated that it is a "state of conduct which is distressing and painful to another."[19] Ironically, it went on to state that in light of the above exposition, Arvind Singh did not do anything that could be said to be 'cruel'. The Bench also stated that in the absence of any linkage established with dowry and any *other* evidence of torture, a case under section 498-A could not be made out against the accused.

Frequency of Cruelty- a necessary factor

In several cases of matrimonial cruelty, Courts have applied unreasonable standards in assessing the gravity of acts that may qualify as cruelty within the meaning of section 498-A. While emphasizing that the frequency of cruelty is a necessary factor in determining its sufficiency under section 498-A, they have ended up going to the extent of normalizing violence. In many of these decisions, gravity is equated with frequency of abuse and in the absence of exponentials that judges find acceptable, singular episodes are discarded as non-serious events. Courts have consistently treated family-based violence against women as part of the "ordinary wear and tear of life".[20] The cases of

[19] *Supra* note 18.

[20] Naveen Kohli v. Neetu Kohli, A.I.R. 2006 S.C. 1675 (India); Savitri Pandey v. Prem Chandra Pandey, (2002) 2 S.C.C. 73 (India); Samar Ghosh v. Jaya Ghosh, (2007) 4 S.C.C. 511 (India).

Girdhar Shankar Tawade v State of Maharashtra,[21] and *Gopal v State of Rajasthan*,[22] are worthy of exploration from this perspective.

Gopal's case, which also involved an unnatural death of a young woman, the SC upheld the Trial Court's verdict that a 'single act of cruelty' is not sufficient to attract the penalty under section 498-A. This judgment of the SC resonated with the judges subsequently giving the verdict Girdhar Shankar Tawade's case,[23] where it was held that unless the Prosecution is able to prove beyond reasonable doubt that a *series of acts* amounting to cruelty were inflicted on the victim, a case under section 498-A cannot be made out. Despite the testimony of witnesses to the effect that on a number of occasions they had visited the deceased's house and had requested the husband to refrain from harassing her, the Court held that in the absence of a demand for dowry, the facts were not sufficient to constitute matrimonial cruelty within the definition of section 498-A.

In fact, this problematic sentiment of the Court was echoed as far as two decades back, in *Richhpal Kaur v State of Haryana*,[24] where the SC had stated that frequency of violence is a necessary factor in judging its relevance under section 498-A of the IPC.

Misconstruing Dowry

While harassment for dowry can be brought within the statutory meaning of matrimonial cruelty, section 498-A is often wrongly presumed as a provision which mandates the presence of dowry harassment for conviction. Consequently, while in few cases like the ones discussed earlier, Courts have tried to find direct or oblique references to dowry, in other cases, they have refused to accept the presence of cruelty by altering the meaning of 'dowry'. For example, in 2007, the SC delivered an evasive judgment in the case of *Appasaheb and Anr. v State of Maharashtra*,[25] in which the victim, two and a half years into her marriage, was found dead due to insecticide poisoning. The judgment stated that "a demand for money on account of some financial

[21] Girdhar Shankar Tawade v. State of Maharashtra, (2002) 5 S.C.C. 177 (India).
[22] Gopal v. State of Rajasthan, A.I.R. 2005 S.C. 222 (India).
[23] *Supra* note 21.
[24] Richhpal Kaur v. State of Haryana, (1990) 2 R.C.R. 18 (India).
[25] Appasaheb v. State of Maharashtra, (2007) 9 S.C.C. 721 (India).

stringency or for meeting some urgent domestic expenses or for purchasing manure cannot be termed as a demand for dowry as the said word is normally understood."[26]

In the same year, in a similar case of dowry death, the only evidence available in the form of a dying declaration and letters exchanged between the victim and her mother. The dying declaration had been made by the victim to her father in the presence of other relatives, where she stated that her mother-in-law, who was the accused, had set her on fire while she was cooking in the kitchen. However, the SC dismissed the existence of matrimonial cruelty, *inter alia*, on the ground that the letters were written by the victim three years prior to her death.[27] The letters stated that the accused was embarrassed that the victim's family had not incurred a certain amount of expenditure despite promising to do so, and that victim's husband was planning to contract a second marriage.[28] Although the Trial Court and the High Court had considered the content of these letters as relevant facts and convicted the accused based on the available evidence, the SC adopted the principle of literal interpretation while analyzing the language of the letters,[29] and stated that the mother-in-law's displeasure at the amount of expenditure incurred by the victim's family cannot be equated to a demand for dowry by her.[30] On this ground, the accused was acquitted from her liability under section 498-A. In its legal reasoning, the SC also went on to say that section 498-A does not specifically speak of dowry and that the victim's letters were not sufficient "material evidence" to infer that she was harassed by her mother-in-law to meet any "unlawful demand for property", as was the requirement in the second limb of the explanation to this section.[31]

Subsequently, in *Ran Singh v. State of Haryana and Anr*,[32] while reversing the order of conviction of the accused, a two-judge bench consisting of Justice P. Sathasivam and

---

[26] *Id.*
[27] Shivanand Mallappa Koti v. State of Karnataka, (2007) S.C.C. 2314 (India).
[28] *Id.*
[29] *Id.*
[30] *Id.*
[31] *Id.*
[32] Ran Singh v. State of Haryana, A.I.R. 2008 S.C. 1294 (India).

Justice Dr Arijit Pasayat noted that "customary payments" cannot be considered as dowry.[33]

Marital Rape: Grievous Hurt but not Matrimonial Cruelty

Matrimonial Cruelty has several manifestations and marital rape is a common variation. In India, rape of a wife by her husband is not recognized as an offence. In this regard, a legitimate question which arises is whether the present definition of matrimonial cruelty in section 498-A may include marital rape in its ambit. Under section 498-A, an act amounts to matrimonial cruelty if it causes grave injury to a woman's life or limb or to her physical or mental health. Hence, the fact of marital rape, when proved, is sufficient to qualify as matrimonial cruelty. However, certain judgments by Indian courts reveal otherwise. The case of Bomma Ilaiah,[34] is one in point. The case of the Prosecution was that the accused forced his wife to have sexual intercourse with her, and in the process, inserted sticks into her vagina causing severe injuries. As a consequence of this, she bled profusely and even fell unconscious. Although the Trial Court had convicted the accused under section 498-A as well as section 325 of the IPC, the High Court interestingly acquitted the perpetrator. Ironically, the Court concluded that the evidence was sufficient to convict the accused of Grievous Hurt but did not constitute matrimonial cruelty under section 498-A. The fact that marital rape of the victim and serious injuries to her private parts are, by themselves, sufficient to show matrimonial cruelty under section 498-A was not accepted by the court.

Continuing Confusion: Exceptional deviations

Although the Supreme Court and High Courts have shown difficulty in their appreciation of the meaning of cruelty under section 498-A, and have sometimes discarded available evidence on the grounds that they were insufficient, the concept of cruelty has undergone mutations favourable to the victim. However, while being of use to individual victims, these cases have added to the confusion arising from the inconsistent interpretation of matrimonial cruelty.

---

[33] *Id*; Satvir Singh v. State of Punjab, (2001) 8 S.C.C. 633 (India).
[34] Bomma Ilaiah v. State of A.P., 2003 CriLJ 2439 (India).

For instance, in Mohd Hoshan's case, the SC agreed with the Andhra Pradesh High Court's contextual interpretation of the term "cruelty" in the case of Mohd. Hoshan.[35] In this case, the Trial Court had held that taunting and scolding the victim for the way she cooked or commenting on her looks could not be sufficient to drive a woman to commit suicide. However, the High Court set aside the order of the Trial Court by stating that cruelty cannot be guided by any standard objective parameters.[36] It is a subjective factor and can vary from one person to another. Apart from that, the High Court also took note of the fact that while the victim was getting burned, the accused and his family did not make any effort to save her, despite the fact that they were present near her. The SC upheld the verdict of the High Court but modified the sentence of imprisonment to the period already undergone.

Along the same lines, in an earlier case,[37] the SC had stated that taunting a married woman for not bringing sufficient dowry and calling her ugly constitutes harassment and torture and that such acts constitute cruelty within the meaning of section 498-A.[38]

A comparison of Hoshan's case with the preceding case discussed above reflects the inconsistencies in interpreting cruelty under section 498A. As rightly pointed out by the Andhra Pradesh High Court and the SC, whether or not a given set of facts qualifies as sufficient cruelty within the meaning of section 498-A cannot be verified by an objective assessment. The Trial Court's outright rejection of the possibility that verbal abuse has the potential to drive a woman to commit suicide, as was done in Hoshan's case, is a concrete example of the approach of courts towards violence in marriages. Likewise, the emphasis of the SC in Tawade's case on the requirement of a "series of acts" for cruelty to have occurred deviates from the basic objective and requirement of section 498A.

On the issue of what matters may constitute matrimonial cruelty, the case of Bhaskarlal,[39] is significant. In 2009, the SC had adjudicated that charges under section 498-A cannot be filed against the parents-in-law by the daughter-in-law merely because

---

[35] Mohd. Hoshan v. State of A.P., (2002) 7 S.C.C. 414 (India).
[36] *Id.*
[37] Pawan Kumar v. State of Haryana, (1996) 4 S.C.C. 17 (India).
[38] *Id.*
[39] Bhaskarlal v. Monica, (2014) 3 S.C.C. 383 (India).

the Prosecution was able to prove that they had "kicked" the victim. Four years later, in 2013, the SC recalled its verdict and held that it is not necessary to connect every case of cruelty with dowry harassment for penal sanctions under section 498-A to be attracted. Hence, a case of physically harassing the daughter-in-law by kicking and threatening her with a divorce cannot be *prima facie* rejected at the threshold. On the basis of this judgment, the stay order on section 498-A proceedings against Bhaskarlal and his wife was lifted and the SC asked for expeditious disposal of the case considering the loss of time.

Unreasonable Doubts, 'Insufficient' Evidence and Consequent Acquittals

In many cases, the reason for an acquittal under section 498-A is that courts do not find sufficient evidence to establish the guilt of the accused. Since the nature of matrimonial cruelty is such that it happens within the privacy of family, most of the evidence is circumstantial. Circumstantial evidence is indirect in nature and therefore, it does not prove the fact in question directly but establishes other facts from which the point in question may be inferred conclusively and satisfactorily.[40] In terms of the weight or quality of evidence, there is hardly any difference between direct and circumstantial evidence.[41] But circumstantial evidence is ignored by courts and is often discounted as insufficient. When combined with other requirements of an accusatorial mechanism, it creates insurmountable barriers for the victim as the question of what constitutes sufficient evidence continues to elude the prosecution.

For example, in M Srinivasulu's case,[42] the Trial Court had convicted the accused under section 304-B read with section 498-A. The victim was a young girl who had died of 100 percent burn injuries after being immolated. Although the conviction was initially made by the Sessions Court after examining 11 witnesses and 16 documents, on appeal, the High Court acquitted the mother-in-law, who was the co-accused in this case. The conviction of the husband was upheld by the High Court, although his sentence was

---

[40] M. Srinivasulu v. State of Andhra Pradesh, A.I.R. 2007 S.C. 3146 (India).
[41] *Id.*
[42] *Supra* note 40.

reduced. However, the SC ultimately acquitted the accused. His acquittal was based primarily on three letters in which the victim had stated that she was not happy in the marriage but had not mentioned anything against her husband. A reading of the case does not indicate why the SC felt the need to re-appreciate facts and evidence even though the Sessions Court and the High Court had already established the guilt of the accused.

Adding to the list of cases resulting in acquittals under section 498-A is the case of Sukhram.[43] The trial court had convicted both the accused under section 498-A and section 304-B. It was proved beyond reasonable doubt by the prosecution that: (i) the deceased was constantly harassed by her in-laws after marriage, (ii) that her dead body was recovered from a well within a year of her marriage, (iii) that the cause of the death was not drowning but ante-mortem by throttling and asphyxiation, indicating that she had been murdered, and (iv) although the accused had taken the plea of alibi, upon cross-examination of the mother-in-law of the deceased, it was clearly established that they were present at home during the said occurrence. Despite all these facts being proven, the High Court held that the facts were not sufficient to establish a case of section 498-A or section 304-B, while simultaneously convicting them for murder under section 302. The High Court constantly emphasized on the absence of an eye-witness but eventually, found the chain of circumstantial evidence to be complete. Ultimately, in the SC, the father-in-law, who was the co-accused, was found to be not guilty under any of the sections and his order of conviction was set aside. It was held that he could have at best been present during the commission of the crime but there was nothing to suggest that he even had the knowledge of the crime being committed. Further, the fact that the charge of murder was not framed against him and he was still convicted by the High Court was another reason for his acquittal. A complete reading of the case suggests that both the accused were acquitted of charges under section 498-A, although one of the accused, (i.e.) the husband, was also convicted for murder, which was not set aside

[43] Sukhram v. State of Maharashtra, A.I.R. 2007 S.C. 3050 (India).

by the SC. It is difficult to comprehend how the husband could be convicted for murder but still be acquitted of matrimonial cruelty.

Sometimes courts have expected unreasonably high standard of precision and exactness to determine whether the victim was subjected to cruelty under section 498-A. In the case of Amar Singh,[44] the High Court of Rajasthan as well as the SC acquitted two of the accused (parents-in-law) of charges under section 304-B as well as section 498-A. The acquittal, *inter-alia*, was based on the fact that the Prosecution Witness was not able to state the exact nature of harassment and torture that was meted out to the deceased by the parents-in-law. Contrary to its decisions in cases such as Pawan Kumar,[45] and Mohd Hoshan,[46] the SC stated that it is not sufficient to state in court that the deceased was taunted, criticized and harassed by the parents-in-law for not being able to bring a scooter or cash. In the Court's opinion, the fact that the Prosecution was not able to clearly establish the content of the harassment or nature of the torture left space for a benefit of doubt in favour of the accused.

As if to add insult to injury, the two-judge bench of the SC, in this case, even cited Kans Raj's case,[47] to indicate that in such cases, there exists a tendency to rope in parents and other relatives of the husband as co-accused, which should be actively discouraged.[48]

Cruelty, Standard of Proof and the Relevance of Context

In India, there exists an undue emphasis on the fundamental principle of establishing a case beyond reasonable doubt. The necessity to arrest this trend has been echoed by the judiciary on several occasions. In the case of Shivaji Sahabrao Bobade,[49] Justice V.R. Krishna Iyer declared unequivocally that a misplaced emphasis on this principle is antithetical to the idea of justice.[50] In *Sucha Singh and Anr. v State of Punjab*,[51] the SC

---

[44] Amar Singh v. State of Rajasthan, (2010) 9 S.C.C. 64 (India).
[45] *Supra* note 36.
[46] *Supra* note 34.
[47] Kans Raj v. State of Punjab, (2000) 5 S.C.C. 207 (India).
[48] *Id.*
[49] Shivaji Sahabrao Bobade v. State of Maharashtra, (1973) S.C.C. (Cri) 1033 (India).
[50] *Id.*
[51] Sucha Singh v. State of Punjab, (2003) 7 S.C.C. 643 (India).

held that exaggerated devotion to the plea of benefit of doubt and blind adherence to the principle of letting a hundred guilty persons free frustrates the objective of justice.[52] Likewise, in 2011, in the case of *Iqbal Moosa Patel v State of Gujarat*,[53] while deciding a case of contraband, the SC held that the degree of proof required under the phrase 'beyond reasonable doubt' is not one where the prosecution has to establish the case beyond a "shadow of doubt."[54] Incidentally, 2011 was also the year in which the decision of Arnesh Kumar,[55] was passed by the SC. While on one hand, courts were emphasizing upon a liberal approach towards the standard of proof in criminal cases, on the other hand, battered women were facing the consequence of misapplication of the principle of beyond reasonable doubt in cases of matrimonial cruelty.

Despite the liberal interpretation of the concept of 'beyond reasonable doubt', criminal cases filed under section 498-A of the IPC lean in favour of the accused on most occasions. In the absence of strong evidence, which is common in such cases due to the nature of offences, it becomes even more difficult for the victim to secure the ends of justice. An analysis of leading judgments of the SC in this area reveals that judges expect the victim to prove her case beyond any 'shadow of doubt' and not just beyond reasonable doubt. This approach has led courts to arrive at bizarre conclusions using flawed methods, such as questioning the sufficiency of cruelty against victims even when the accused's conduct results in homicide, rejecting available circumstantial evidence and lamenting on the unavailability of primary evidence, interpreting terms without appreciating the context and legislative intent of the legislation, and finally, as a cumulative impact of the above factors, demonizing a well-crafted legislation designed to protect vulnerable women.

Courts have failed to note that in an accusatorial mechanism where the Prosecution must prove its case beyond reasonable doubt, this burden is a heavy one to discharge as violence against women in marriages takes place in the privacy of homes. In most

---

[52] *Id.*
[53] Iqbal Moosa Patel v. State of Gujarat, (2011) 2 S.C.C. 198 (India).
[54] *Id.*
[55] *Supra* note 18.

Indian families, the victim's position may be further weakened by the fact that marriages are generally virilocal. The factor of privacy combined with incompetence, indolence and corruption of investigating agencies makes the entire process even more complicated for the victim. The SC has noted and reiterated this in several cases including the case of Arvind Singh.[56]

Under such circumstances, misunderstanding the concept of 'beyond reasonable doubt' as beyond any doubt whatsoever leads to miscarriage of justice and impairs the faith of victims in the criminal justice system, who then choose to suffer in silence or revoke their rights by not approaching courts. These acquittals ultimately create numerical data which counts against the victim and forms a basis for adverse propaganda against important legal provisions such as section 498-A. Therefore, for the victims to escape this endless cycle of systemic re-victimization, it is high time that courts reassessed their understanding and interpretation of violence in intimate relationships such as marriage.

Conclusion

To conclude, while it may be true that the number of acquittals in cases of section 498A may be high, it is important to assess the reasons underlying these acquittals. While many of these acquittals may be the result of a bad investigation by the police, many more could be a consequence of interpretational and evidentiary errors in decision-making. In none of these circumstances would it be fair for victims to pay the price by being labelled as insincere, incredulous or dishonest. What needs to be reassessed is not whether Indian women still need the strength of section 498-A to protect them in their matrimonial homes, but whether courts can do better by avoiding pitfalls of the legal process arising from a glaring gap between the crime and its context.

---

[56] *Supra* note 18.

UNLEASHING THE POWER OF COLLECTIVE BARGAINING: STRATEGIES FOR EFFECTIVE NEGOTIATION IN TODAY'S WORKPLACE

DR. JAYKUMAR BHONGALE*
MR. OISHIK BHATTACHARYA**

ABSTRACT

Development relies on peace, as conflicts drain valuable time, energy, and resources from society. However, conflicts are inevitable in practicality. Traditional court processes for dispute resolution are often lengthy, affecting commerce, business, administration, and development work. Alternative methods like collective bargaining, conciliation, mediation, arbitration, worker participation in management, and wage boards have emerged as ways to navigate this maze of litigation. Among these options, collective bargaining is often considered the most effective approach, as it allows disputing parties to come together and resolve their differences in a respectful and amicable manner.

The growth of industrial relations plays a crucial role in a nation's pursuit of balancing competitiveness, fair pay, and improved working conditions. A healthy labor market is essential for current and future economic growth, as well as the welfare of workers and their families. Collective bargaining, as a dynamic process or institution for negotiating terms and conditions of employment, is influenced by changes in the macroeconomic environment and political developments.

The purpose and scope of collective bargaining have naturally evolved in the context of liberalization. Employers, their organizations, and trade unions often engage in collective bargaining as a means to foster strong working relationships based on respect and understanding. According to the ILO Constitution and the 1998 ILO Declaration on Fundamental Principles and Rights at Work, collective bargaining is recognized as a fundamental right. In addition to improving worker incomes, enhancing working conditions, reducing inequality, and ensuring fair employment relations, collective bargaining has also played a foundational role in democracy and served as a catalyst for workplace innovation. This chapter focuses on the concept of collective bargaining as a whole, considering relevant cases decided by the Top Court, provisions of the Industrial Disputes Act, Trade Union Act, Standing Order, and the Constitution to support the legality of collective bargaining. Furthermore, the various stages of collective bargaining and their interrelation with labor relations maintenance are briefly explained.

Despite its significance, collective bargaining, as the desired method of industrial bargaining, has been marginalized in the past due to political factors. However, it has been recognized for its contributions to Indian industries, bringing about changes in labor relations and facilitating restructuring in both the public and private sectors in response to the country's evolving economic climate.

Keywords- Collective Bargaining, Negotiation, Labour Relations, Trade Union

INTRODUCTION

According to the definition given under Article 2 of the Collective Bargaining Convention, 1981 (No. 154), collective bargaining "extends to all negotiations which take place between an employer, a group of employers or one or more employers' organizations, on the one hand, and one or more workers' organizations, on the other, for:

(a) Determining working conditions and terms of employment; and/or

(b) Regulating relations between employers and workers; and/or

(c) Regulating relations between employers or their organizations and a workers' organization or workers' organizations".[57]Collective bargaining is made up of two words: collective, which means united or a group action, and bargaining, which means to negotiate. So, put together, it means collective or group bargaining.

---

*Assistant Professor and Research coordinator of Bharati Vidyapeeth Deemed to be University, New Law College, Pune.

** Student of BBA LLB SEM VII, Bharati Vidyapeeth, Deemed to be University, New Law College.

[57] *Convention C154 - Collective Bargaining Convention, 1981 (No. 154)*. (n.d.). https://www.ilo.org/dyn/normlex/en/f?p=NORMLEXPUB:12100:0::NO::P12100_INSTRUMENT_ID:312299.

In essence, negotiation is a lifelong activity. We bargain every single day. Sometimes it's for trivial things, and other times it might be for a significant occasion.

Negotiation can be defined: "...as attempting, through discussion, persuasion and where appropriate, compromise to reach an agreement with the other party(s) on a particular issue or range of issues."[58]

Effective negotiation is a technique used to resolve conflicts. It is a method for arriving at a compromise or agreement while averting conflict and argument.

STAGES OF COLLECTIVE BARGAINING

The stages of collective bargaining include the following:

1. **Creation Of A Union**

   Section 9A of the Trade Unions Act of 1926 states that seven workers are the minimum needed to establish a union. Although it is not necessary to join a union, there are advantages to doing so. These advantages include giving employees the proper representation they need, allowing them to use money for specific goals, and providing them with protection from legal action.

2. **Charter of Demands**

   A collective bargaining process can now be initiated by either the union or the business. The labor union then meets with each of its members in turn to draft a charter of demands.

3. **Negotiation**

   A demand charter is submitted to start the negotiation process. During the first meeting, the union often presents formal requests for amendments to the current collective bargaining agreements. The chance for counter-proposals is then given to the management. Until they come to an agreement, this will continue.

4. **Strikes**

---

[58] *Collective Bargaining and Negotiation Skills*. (2003). Retrieved February 22, 2023, from https://www.ilo.org/wcmsp5/groups/public/---asia/---ro-bangkok/---ilo jakarta/documents/publication/wcms_120206.pdf.

The union has the right to declare a strike if talks break down. Section 22 of the Industrial Disputes Act states that public utility workers must give six weeks' notice before going on strike and may do so up to fourteen days later. While the conciliation procedure is ongoing and for seven days following its conclusion, management and the union are not permitted to engage in any form of industrial action.[59]

MAINTENANCE OF LABOUR RELATIONS

The collective bargaining process enables the expression of the interests of both employers and employees, the identification of shared interests, the balancing of various interests, and the negotiation of trade-offs. For instance, collective bargaining has been utilised in some countries to balance business demands for flexible work schedules and a decrease in overtime costs with worker demands for a work-life balance. The conclusion of collective negotiations is more likely to be seen as fair and more equal than those reached through individual bargaining or unilateral contracting as a result of engaging in a process of bargaining in good faith. This is advantageous for businesses in terms of employee dedication, stability, and productivity as well as for employees in terms of better pay and working conditions. Workers typically obtain a larger proportion of productivity improvements as wages through collective bargaining. This can then encourage teamwork, boost productivity inside the company, and support stronger economic demand. By offering a formalised and accepted method of conflict management, collective bargaining enhances the environment for labour relations. During the term of the collective agreement, peace clauses may be included. Collective agreements often provide grievance procedures. This may lead to more dependable and healthy working relationships. The laws governing labour relations are made valid by collective bargaining. The likelihood of compliance with the terms and conditions of

[59] *Collective Bargaining and Negotiation Skills*. (2003). Retrieved February 22, 2023, from https://www.ilo.org/wcmsp5/groups/public/---asia/---ro-bangkok/---ilo-jakarta/documents/publication/wcms_120206.pdf.

employment and work is higher where they have been negotiated. Through collective bargaining, the parties can create a collective agreement that is specific to their business or industry and governs the employment relationship. Parties can also use it to resolve issues that could be unique to their line of business or industry. Parties are known to draft contracts that may help the business adjust during a downturn or introduce technology and organisational change in a way that safeguards employees from risk and produces the intended results.[60]

PRINCIPLES OF COLLECTIVE BARGAINING

<u>For the management and union:</u>

1. Collective bargaining should be turned into both a learning and negotiating process. It should give trade union leaders a chance to discuss with management the needs, wants, complaints, and attitudes of its workers and allow management to explain to union leaders and, through them, to employees, the economic issues it is facing.
2. Both the management and the union must view collective bargaining as a way to find the best possible solution, not as a way to get the most while giving up the least. Instead of settling for a compromise, a problem must be solved in an honest effort.

<u>For the Management:</u>

1. All of the management's representatives must accept and uphold the development and implementation of a realistic labor policy.
2. The management must recognize the trade union without any conditions and accept it as a positive force in the business. Only then will the trade union feel secure in its position within the organization or factory.

---

[60] *Q&As on business and collective bargaining*. (2012, February 1). https://www.ilo.org/empent/areas/business-helpdesk/faqs/WCMS_DOC_ENT_HLP_CB_FAQ_EN/lang--en/index.htm#Q2.

3. The management shouldn't take the goodwill of the workforce for granted. It should periodically review the laws and ordinances that govern its labor force. It will be able to ascertain the attitudes of its employees in this way, as well as to make them more comfortable and win their cooperation and goodwill.

4. The management should act on the presumption that the trade union must be treated fairly in order to become a responsible and conservative organization. Additionally, it should build a strong enough rapport with the union and its representatives so that they won't take any action that could endanger that relationship lightly.

5. There should be just one union in the company that the management deals with. No negotiations should begin with one of the two trade unions seeking recognition until one of them can prove that a majority of the employees are members of the organization.

For Trade Union:

1. Trade unions must eradicate extortion and other anti-democratic practices from their own ranks in light of the rights granted to organized labor.

2. Because their demands are typically covered by the earnings and resources of the company where their members are employed, trade union leaders are aware of the economic implications of collective bargaining.

3. Trade union leaders should support the elimination of any restrictions that are likely to raise prices, lower the amount that can be paid out in wages, and lead to low employment and, in the long run, a lower standard of living for all societal groups.

LAWS GOVERNING TRADE UNIONS

In India, both federal and state laws guarantee the freedom to organize a union, join one, and engage in collective bargaining:

1. The Constitution of India,1950- The fundamental right to freedom of speech and expression is outlined in Article 19(1)(c) of the Constitution of India, 1950

("Constitution").The right "to form associations or unions," including trade unions, is also guaranteed to India's citizens under the freedom of expression.

According to the SC, joining an association or union is also a part of the freedoms guaranteed by Article 19(1) (c). The State has the right to impose reasonable limitations on this right. Article 19(1) (c) of the Constitution recognizes the following freedoms as fundamental rights:

1. The right to meet;
2. The right to travel;
3. The right to express their opinions and discuss their problems; and
4. The right to own property.[61]

2. The Trade Unions Act, 1926- The Trade Unions Act of 1926 (the "TU Act") defines certain legal requirements for registered trade unions and allows for the formation and registration of trade unions. Trade unions are "any combinations, whether temporary or permanent, formed primarily for the purpose of regulating the relations between workmen and employers, between workmen and employers, or for imposing restrictive conditions on the conduct of any trade or business," according to the TU Act. This definition includes any federation or two or more trade unions. Every employee has the option to join a union or decline to do so. However, not all labor unions can be categorized as labor organizations. The voluntary "Code of Discipline" and the "Criteria for Recognition of Unions" appended to the Code were adopted by the Standing Labour Committee in its 16th session in 1957 and subsequently ratified by the representatives of Employers and CTUOs at the 16th session of the Indian Labour Conference, held in 1958. At the moment, recognition of trade unions operating in industrial establishments is governed by these provisions. The Code is a set of rules that all parties have mutually and voluntarily agreed upon to uphold discipline in business, in both the public and

[61] The Constitution of India, 1950.https://legislative.gov.in/constitution-of-india.

private sectors. The management agrees to recognize the Union in accordance with the criteria developed in the Code, according to Clause III (vii) of the Code.[62]

3. The Industrial Disputes Act, 1947- The IDA regulates the rights of employers and employees in the investigation and resolution of industrial disputes in a manner that also addresses trade unions. It allows for collective bargaining through negotiation and mediation and, in the event of failure, either voluntary arbitration or mandatory adjudication with the active involvement of trade unions. According to the IDA55, a settlement reached through collective bargaining is legally binding. There are two distinct settlement types:

   i. Settlements reached during conciliation proceedings before the authority; these agreements bind both members and non-members of the signatory union as well as all current and future management employees.

   ii. Settlements that are reached outside of conciliation proceedings but are signed independently by the parties thereto; these settlements only bind the signatories or parties thereto.[63]

LANDMARK JUDGMENTS

1. **UK Ltd v. Dunkley and others**[64]- The claimants worked as shop floor or manual laborers for Kostal and were Unite members. A non-binding Recognition and Procedural Agreement establishing a process for collective bargaining was signed by Kostal and Unite in February 2015.

Unite and Kostal started formally negotiating a change to annual pay in October 2015. Kostal's offer was put to a vote of union members in December. The majority of voters—nearly 80%—voted against it. The same offer was then made directly to the staff by

---

[62] The Trade Unions Act, 1926, 16.https://labour.gov.in/sites/default/files/TheTradeUnionsAct1926.pdf.

[63] The Industrial Disputes Act, 1947,14. https://labour.gov.in/sites/default/files/THEINDUSTRIALDISPUTES_ACT1947_0.pdf.

[64] (Kostal UK Ltd v. Dunkley & Ors *[2021] UKSC 47 (26 October 2021)*, n.d.).

Kostal, who threatened to withhold their Christmas bonus if they did not accept by a specific deadline. It's important to note that this offer avoided the conciliation stage of the agreed-upon collective bargaining procedure.91% of those who were qualified to accept the offer had done so by January. The remaining employees received a similar offer from Kostal at the end of January, with a warning that failure to accept it could result in the termination of their employment agreements with notice. Kostal and Unite came to a collective bargaining agreement in November 2016 that was largely in line with the original proposal.

It was decided that the employer (Kostal) violated section 145B of the Trade Union and Labour Relations (Consolidation) Act 1992 (the "1992 Act") by directly approaching workers with offers to alter their terms and conditions of employment and avoiding the collective bargaining process established with Unite the Union ("Unite").

2. **Karnal Leather Karamchari Sanghatan (Regd.) v. Respondent: Liberty Footwear Company (Regd.) and Ors[65]**- The Court held that the Industrial Disputes Act of 1947 aims to achieve social justice through collective bargaining. The system of justice distribution in industrial adjudication includes voluntary arbitration. As a result, the arbitrator is one of the numerous statutory tribunals. When a dispute is referred to arbitration, it is imperative that the employees are informed of the dispute and the arbitrator whose decision will ultimately bind them. They need to be aware of what is being arbitrated, who their arbitrator is, and what is in store for them. They need to have the chance to discuss their opinions with one another and, if necessary, bring them before the arbitrator. The Union only aids employees in resolving their conflicts with management; however, it is the employees' responsibility to make decisions and suggest solutions in the end. Therefore, in our opinion, the arbitration agreement must be made public

[65] Karnal Leather Karamchari Sanghatan (Regd.) v. Respondent: Liberty Footwear Company (Regd.) and Ors (1989)4 SCC 448.

before the arbitrator decides whether to rule on the merits of the dispute. The arbitral award would be rendered null and void if this condition were not met.

CONCLUSION

Collective bargaining is a key means through which employers and their organizations and trade unions can establish fair wages and working conditions. Additionally, it offers the framework for healthy labour relations. Wages, working hours, training, workplace health and safety, and fair treatment are common problems on the negotiation table. To reach a collective agreement that governs the terms and conditions of employment is the goal of these negotiations. The rights and obligations of the parties may also be covered by collective agreements, promoting harmonious and effective workplaces and industries. A crucial strategy for lowering inequality and boosting labour protection is to make collective bargaining and agreements more inclusive.

Exploring the Intersection of Law and Ethics in the Age of AI, Robotics, and Algorithms

Dr. JayKumar Bhongale[66]
Ms. Saheli Chakraborty[67]

Abstract

Artificial Intelligence, Robotics, and Algorithms have become crucial aspects of our everyday lives, affecting everything from healthcare and education to transportation and entertainment. But with great power comes great responsibility, and as these technologies continue to evolve, so do the legal and ethical issues surrounding them. In this article, we will explore the legal and ethical landscape of AI, Robotics, and Algorithms, both in India and internationally. We will discuss the key challenges that arise in this field and provide insights into how these challenges are being addressed by policymakers and industry leaders.

1. Introduction to AI, Robotics, and Algorithms

Artificial Intelligence (AI), robotics, and algorithms are technologies that are changing the way we live, work, and interact with each other. AI is the ability of machines to perform tasks that normally require human intelligence, such as visual perception, speech recognition, decision-making, and language translation. Robotics refers to the design, construction, and operation of robots, which are machines that can perform tasks autonomously or with minimal human intervention. Algorithms are sets of

[66] Assistant Professor at BVDU New Law College, Pune
[67] Author is a student of BVDU New Law College, Pune

instructions that tell a computer what to do, and they are used in a wide range of applications, from search engines to financial trading systems. [68]

AI, robotics, and algorithms have the potential to create enormous benefits for society, including increased efficiency, improved safety, and enhanced quality of life. However, they also raise significant legal and ethical challenges, such as the risk of bias, discrimination, and privacy violations. In this blog post, we will explore the legal and ethical landscape of AI, robotics, and algorithms, both in India and abroad. We will examine the key issues and debates surrounding these technologies, and we will consider the ways in which policymakers, businesses, and individuals can navigate these challenges.

2. Legal and ethical concerns

The increasing use of AI, robotics, and algorithms has raised several legal and ethical concerns. From a legal perspective, issues such as data privacy, data security, and liability arise. There is a need for a clear legal framework to regulate the use of these technologies and ensure that they are used responsibly and ethically. Countries such as India have introduced data protection laws to safeguard the privacy of individuals and regulate the collection, storage, and use of personal data.[69] Similarly, the European Union's General Data Protection Regulation (GDPR) has set out strict rules for the processing of personal data.

From an ethical perspective, concerns such as bias, transparency, and accountability arise. AI systems are only as unbiased as the data they are fed, and this can lead to

[68] 'Ethics of Artificial Intelligence', , *Wikipedia* (2023) <https://en.wikipedia.org/w/index.php?title=Ethics_of_artificial_intelligence&oldid=1149303528> accessed 12 April 2023.

[69] Mark Ryan and Bernd Carsten Stahl, 'Artificial Intelligence Ethics Guidelines for Developers and Users: Clarifying Their Content and Normative Implications' (2020) 19 Journal of Information, Communication and Ethics in Society 61 <https://doi.org/10.1108/JICES-12-2019-0138> accessed 12 April 2023.

unintended consequences. For example, facial recognition technology has been shown to produce more errors when identifying individuals of certain races or genders. It is important to ensure that AI systems are designed to be transparent and that users can understand how decisions are made. Additionally, there must be accountability for the decisions made by AI systems, particularly when they have significant impact on individuals or society as a whole.[70]

3. The regulatory landscape in India and abroad

The regulatory landscape surrounding AI, Robotics, and Algorithms is constantly evolving, both in India and abroad. In India, the government has been working on developing a comprehensive regulatory framework for AI and related technologies. In 2020, the National Strategy for Artificial Intelligence was released, outlining the government's vision for AI in India and providing a roadmap for policy development. Additionally, the government has established the Centre of Excellence for Artificial Intelligence, which is tasked with developing AI solutions to address societal challenges.[71]

Internationally, there are several regulatory bodies that are working on developing guidelines and regulations for AI and related technologies. The European Union's General Data Protection Regulation (GDPR) is one such example. The GDPR provides guidelines for the collection, storage, and processing of personal data, which is relevant for AI systems that rely on data for training and decision-making.

Furthermore, the International Organization for Standardization (ISO) has developed a set of standards for AI systems, which cover areas such as ethics, privacy, and

---

[70] ibid.

[71] 'How AI, Robotics, and Automation Change the Landscape of Employment?' <https://www.analyticsinsight.net/how-ai-robotics-and-automation-change-the-landscape-of-employment/> accessed 12 April 2023.

transparency. These standards provide a framework for companies and organizations to develop AI systems that are safe, ethical, and transparent.[72]

It is important for organizations to stay informed about the regulatory landscape surrounding AI, Robotics, and Algorithms, both in India and abroad. By doing so, they can ensure that their systems are compliant with relevant regulations and standards, and that they are operating ethically and responsibly.

4. Understanding the legal and ethical implications of AI, robotics, and algorithms

The integration of AI, robotics, and algorithms into our daily lives has brought forth a myriad of ethical and legal implications that must be thoroughly understood. One of the primary concerns is the potential for bias and discrimination, as machines are only as unbiased as the data that is fed into them. As such, it is important to ensure that the data used to train AI systems is diverse and representative of all groups in society.

Another ethical concern is the potential loss of jobs as automation becomes more prevalent. It is important to consider the impact of these technologies on the workforce and to develop strategies for upskilling and reskilling workers to ensure they are equipped to thrive in a world where machines are increasingly taking on tasks previously done by humans.[73]

On the legal front, issues such as data privacy, security, and ownership must be carefully considered. The use of personal data to train AI systems must be done in compliance with relevant data protection laws, and individuals must be informed of how their data is being used. Additionally, liability for harm caused by autonomous systems must be clearly defined and allocated.

---

[72] Rob Toews, 'AI Will Transform The Field Of Law' (*Forbes*) <https://www.forbes.com/sites/robtoews/2019/12/19/ai-will-transform-the-field-of-law/> accessed 12 April 2023.

[73] 'Legal & Ethical Aspects of Artificial Intelligence, Robotics & Algorithms' <https://timesofindia.indiatimes.com/readersblog/storyteller/legal-ethical-aspects-of-artificial-intelligence-robotics-algorithms-45346/> accessed 12 April 2023.

Understanding the legal and ethical implications of AI, robotics, and algorithms is crucial for businesses, policymakers, and society as a whole. By considering these implications, we can work towards ensuring that these technologies are developed and deployed in a manner that is both beneficial and responsible.

5. Cases of AI, robotics, and algorithmic bias

Cases of AI, robotics, and algorithmic bias have become increasingly common in recent years, and it's vital that we address these issues to ensure that we're creating a fair and just society. One of the most well-known cases of algorithmic bias was the COMPAS (Correctional Offender Management Profiling for Alternative Sanctions) system used in the US to predict the likelihood of recidivism in criminal offenders.

The system was found to be biased against black defendants, as they were more likely to be classified as having a high risk of recidivism than white defendants with the same criminal history.[74] This highlights the importance of ensuring that algorithms and other forms of AI are designed and tested rigorously to ensure that they are not perpetuating societal biases.

Another example of algorithmic bias is the use of facial recognition technology, which has been found to be less accurate when identifying individuals with darker skin tones. This has serious implications for law enforcement and security agencies, as it could lead to innocent people being wrongly identified and potentially targeted.[75]

In India, there have been cases of AI and robotics being used to discriminate against individuals based on caste and religion. This is a significant issue in a country where discrimination based on these factors is illegal and highlights the need for strict regulation and oversight of the use of these technologies.

---

[74] Hitesh Bhatt and others, 'Artificial Intelligence and Robotics Led Technological Tremors: A Seismic Shift towards Digitizing the Legal Ecosystem' (2022) 12 Applied Sciences 11687 <https://www.mdpi.com/2076-3417/12/22/11687> accessed 12 April 2023.

[75] ibid.

6. How AI, robotics, and algorithms are transforming industries

The rise of AI, robotics, and algorithms has already begun to transform many industries across the globe. From healthcare to finance, logistics to manufacturing, and even creative industries such as music and art, the impact of these technologies is being felt far and wide. In healthcare, for example, AI-powered tools are helping doctors and researchers to detect diseases earlier and with greater accuracy, while in finance, algorithms are being used to analyze vast amounts of data and make predictions about financial markets.[76]

Similarly, in the manufacturing industry, robotics is being used to automate repetitive tasks, increase efficiency and reduce costs, while in logistics, AI is being used to optimize delivery routes and reduce transportation costs.

The creative industries are also benefiting from AI, with algorithms being used to analyze data and create new music and art that would have been impossible just a few years ago.[77]

The impact of AI, robotics, and algorithms on industries is expected to continue to grow in the coming years, with these technologies becoming increasingly sophisticated and capable of performing more complex tasks. However, as these technologies become more prevalent, it is important to consider the legal and ethical implications of their use, to ensure that they are used in a responsible and beneficial way that benefits society as a whole.

7. The changing nature of work due to AI and robotics

[76] 'Recommendation on the Ethics of Artificial Intelligence | UNESCO' <https://www.unesco.org/en/legal-affairs/recommendation-ethics-artificial-intelligence> accessed 12 April 2023.

[77] 'Legal & Ethical Aspects of Artificial Intelligence, Robotics & Algorithms' (n 7).

The advancements in Artificial Intelligence (AI) and Robotics have revolutionized the way we work, bringing both opportunities and challenges. With AI and Robotics, many jobs are becoming automated and repetitive, which will lead to a significant shift in the nature of work.

There is no doubt that AI and Robotics will create new job opportunities, but at the same time, many traditional jobs will become redundant.[78] For example, many manufacturing jobs that were previously done by humans are now being done by robots. This shift will require a new set of skills and expertise, which will need to be developed to meet the demands of these new jobs.

It is also likely that the rise of AI and Robotics will lead to the creation of new industries and sectors that we cannot even imagine today. These new industries will require a new set of skills, which will need to be developed to meet the demands of these new jobs.

The changing nature of work due to AI and Robotics will also have an impact on the workforce. Employees will need to be retrained and reskilled to adapt to the new working environment. This will require significant investment from companies and governments to ensure that the workforce is equipped with the necessary skills to remain competitive in the new era of work.[79]

Therefore, it is important for governments, businesses, and individuals to understand the changing nature of work due to AI and Robotics and take steps to prepare for the future. By doing so, we can ensure that we are well-equipped to navigate the challenges and capitalize on the opportunities that arise from this new era of work.

8. Guidelines for ethical AI development

As the field of artificial intelligence continues to grow and evolve, it's becoming increasingly important to ensure that the development of AI technology is guided by

---

[78] 'Robotics and Law: Key Legal and Regulatory Implications of the Robotics Age (Part I of II) - ScienceDirect' <https://www.sciencedirect.com/science/article/abs/pii/S0267364916300358> accessed 12 April 2023.

[79] 'Robotics, Artificial Intelligence, and the Evolving Nature of Work | SpringerLink' <https://link.springer.com/chapter/10.1007/978-3-030-08277-2_8> accessed 12 April 2023.

ethical considerations. To this end, many organizations and governments have developed guidelines for ethical AI development.

One such example is the "Ethics Guidelines for Trustworthy AI" developed by the European Commission's High-Level Expert Group on Artificial Intelligence. These guidelines outline a set of principles that AI developers should follow to ensure that their technology is transparent, fair, and respects human rights.[80]

Similarly, the Indian government has also recently released its own draft guidelines for responsible AI development. These guidelines emphasize the need for AI systems to be transparent, explainable, and accountable, and also highlight the importance of ensuring that AI does not perpetuate bias or discrimination.[81]

At the heart of these guidelines is a recognition that AI has the potential to significantly impact society and individuals, and that it's crucial to approach its development with a sense of responsibility and accountability. By following these guidelines for ethical AI development, developers can create AI systems that are not only effective and efficient but also socially responsible and aligned with human values.

9. Responsible use of AI, robotics, and algorithms

As the use of AI, robotics, and algorithms continues to grow, there is a need for responsible use of these technologies. Companies and organizations must ensure that these technologies are used ethically and in a way that does not pose any harm to individuals or society as a whole. This includes ensuring that these technologies are not used to discriminate against any particular group of people and that they do not perpetuate existing biases and inequalities.

---

[80] Oishika Banerji, 'Role of Artificial Intelligence in Law' (*iPleaders*, 26 September 2021) <https://blog.ipleaders.in/role-of-artificial-intelligence-in-law/> accessed 12 April 2023.

[81] Darrell M West and John R Allen, 'How Artificial Intelligence Is Transforming the World' (*Brookings*, 24 April 2018) <https://www.brookings.edu/research/how-artificial-intelligence-is-transforming-the-world/> accessed 12 April 2023.

Responsible use of AI, robotics, and algorithms also means being transparent about how these technologies are being used and ensuring that individuals have control over their own data. This includes being clear about what data is being collected, how it is being used, and who has access to it. Companies must also ensure that they are complying with all relevant laws and regulations related to the use of these technologies.

To ensure responsible use of AI, robotics, and algorithms, it is important that companies and organizations prioritize ethics in their decision-making processes. This includes ensuring that ethical considerations are included in the design and development of these technologies and that they are regularly reviewed to ensure they are being used in a responsible and ethical manner. [82] By prioritizing responsible use of AI, robotics, and algorithms, we can ensure that these technologies are used in a way that benefits society as a whole.

10. Conclusion: Striking a balance between innovation and ethics

As we continue to push the boundaries of technology and explore the possibilities of AI, robotics, and algorithms, it is important to keep in mind the ethical considerations that come with these innovations. While they have the potential to revolutionize many industries and improve our lives in countless ways, we must also be mindful of the potential risks and unintended consequences that may arise.

The key to navigating the legal and ethical landscape of AI, robotics, and algorithms is to strike a balance between innovation and ethics. This means developing these technologies in a way that ensures they are safe, reliable, and trustworthy, while also respecting the rights and dignity of all individuals.

In the case of India, the government has taken important steps to address these issues through its National AI Strategy, which emphasizes the importance of promoting the

[82] 'Legal & Ethical Aspects of Artificial Intelligence, Robotics & Algorithms' (n 7).

responsible use of AI and ensuring that it is aligned with the country's cultural and social values.

At the global level, organizations like the IEEE Global Initiative on Ethics of Autonomous and Intelligent Systems have developed important guidelines and standards for the development and deployment of these technologies. Ultimately, the success of AI, robotics, and algorithms will depend on our ability to strike this delicate balance and ensure that these technologies are developed and used in a way that benefits society as a whole. By remaining vigilant and proactive in our approach, we can help ensure that the future of technology is a bright and ethical one.

EXPLORING THE DEBATE ON CRIMINALIZING CORPORATE OFFENCES IN INDIA

DR. JAYKUMAR BHONGALE*

Mr. Oishik bhattacharya**

ABSTRACT

When we think of crime, our minds often conjure up images of murder, theft, robbery, rape, or assault - crimes that are more visible and sensational. However, the narrow perception of crime solely in terms of these violent acts overlooks the reality of economic and corporate offences, commonly known as white collar crimes. These types of crimes are often complex and technical in nature, and do not require physical presence for their commission. According to Australian criminologist John Braithwaite, corporate crimes can be defined as "the conduct of a corporation or its employees, acting on behalf of the corporation, which is prohibited and punishable by law." Corporate crimes have indirect effects on the public, and dealing with them in court can be challenging as determining appropriate penalties for corporations can be perplexing. This paper delves into the position of Indian jurisprudence on corporate offences and the ongoing debate around their decriminalization. The authors also highlight the impact of corporate crimes on the general public and the role of corporate governance in their commission and prevention. The paper sheds light on the fact that corporate offences are not victimless crimes, and their consequences can be far-reaching, affecting not only shareholders and investors but also employees, consumers, and the overall socio-economic fabric of society. The complexities involved in prosecuting corporate crimes and imposing penalties are also discussed, as the technical nature of these offences can make it difficult to hold corporations accountable.

The paper emphasizes the need to recognize the seriousness of corporate offences and to ensure effective deterrence against corporate misconduct. It also explores the concept of decriminalization of corporate offences, considering the pros and cons of such an approach. While some argue that decriminalization may reduce the burden on the criminal justice system and facilitate ease of doing business, others caution against diluting the deterrence effect of criminal sanctions. The role of corporate governance in preventing and addressing corporate offences is also examined, as strong corporate governance practices can play a crucial role in minimizing the risk of corporate misconduct.

In conclusion, this paper highlights the need for a nuanced and balanced approach towards corporate offences in India. It underscores the importance of acknowledging the impact of white collar crimes on society, and the need for effective mechanisms to hold corporations accountable for their actions. The paper calls for further research and discussion on the topic to arrive at a comprehensive and well-informed approach towards addressing corporate offences in India, while upholding the principles of fairness and justice.

Keywords: - Corporate crimes, criminal offence, Corporate Governance, civil wrong, white collar crime.

INTRODUCTION

"The grandeur of thieving falsity is larceny, the fall of cities."[83]

The word crime mostly invokes a tachistoscopical visual of murder, theft, robbery, dacoity, rape or assault etc in our minds and perhaps the most probable reason for this peculiarity is that the above-mentioned activities feel daunting to mankind and are immediately discerned as something morally wrong by our conscience. People collective as a society feel an urge to curb them and therefore these kind of horrendous activities have been penalized by the laws of nation. However the problem with limiting the perception of crime to the conscience is that society fails to acutely acknowledge the white collar crimes specifically economic and corporate offences due to their technical nature and also on the grounds that there is no physical presence required in commission of white collar crimes. These economic miscreants are usually savvier than

*Assistant Professor and Research coordinator of Bharati Vidyapeeth Deemed to be University, New Law College, Pune.

** Student of BBA LLB SEM VII, Bharati Vidyapeeth, Deemed to be University, New Law College Pune.

[83] Justin K. Mcfarlane Beau.

their street crime counterparts. Monetary offenses are undeniably more alarming for general public as enormous companies have become a kind of private government, for their activities and strategies have impact on zillions of individuals and networks. Also not to mention corporations have the ability to influence a region's economy and politics thus making corporate crimes a major problem.[84]

Common public bears financial consequences of corporate and economic crimes, which are largely indirect, such as the loss of resources due to tax evasion and public frauds, which affect spending on public amenities and services. For instance the major capital market scam done by Harshad Mehta in 1992 amounted to total sum of rs.4,000 crores[85] which was followed by another capital market scam done by C R Bhansali that took place in the same time period was of worth rs.1,200 crores resulting in siphoning a sum of total rs.5,200 crores from market. If we take a closer look at the money sanctioned by union government of India for rural development program in the budget of 1992 and then again looking back at money lost in capital market scam, it can be concluded that union government allocated rs.2, 610 crores for rural development program whereas the capital market scam was of worth rs.5, 200 crores which is nearly double of what union government gave for rural development program. Additionally these fiscal affect foundations of small financial backers can endure an extraordinary loss, including mental agony brought about by the deficiency of resources and monetary stability.

AFFECTS OF CORPORATE CRIMES

Earlier in the paper authors gave a mere glimpse of what corporate crimes can do to society and people, for instance people are affected by health and safety concerns resulting from the disregard for regulations, which include industrial operations such as construction sites where passers-by are harmed by risky practises. Residents and people have been killed and injured in explosions, as well as being harmed by toxic chemicals released, the most well-known of which occurred in Bhopal, India where 3000-5000

---

[84] R. Tomasic, *Corporate Crimes and Corporations Law Enforcement Strategies in Australia,* 1/93 Centre Of National Corporate Research 1, 22 (1993).

[85] P. K. Gupta & S. Gupta, *Corporate frauds in India – perceptions and emerging issues*, 22 Journal of Financial Crime 79, 103 (2015).

people were killed and many more were affected by the leak of methylisocyanate in the air.[86]

According to the World Health Organization, more than 138 million people have died as a result of medical negligence, which includes things like hospital workers giving the wrong therapy to patients, injecting the wrong medicine into a victim, and so on. Another sort of hospital negligence is the incorrect and unlawful dumping of medical waste, which causes problems for persons as well as the environment due to its hazardous qualities.[87] As indicated by the World Health Organization (WHO), improper clinical garbage removal (mostly the utilization of tainted hypodermic needles and needles) brought about 21 million diseases of Hepatitis B, 2 million contaminations of Hepatitis C, and 260,000 instances of HIV in the year 2000. White collar crimes were clearly visible during the serious condition of covid-19, many people took advantage of pandemic in pharmaceutical and medical industry which affected the public at large which also raises questions about the government. For instance Himachal PPE Scam is one of the scams in which political parties were also involved in order to profit from the provision of PPE rather than taking remedial actions.[88]

Many places of recreation are likewise affected by white-collar crime. Consumers may suffer financially as a result of having to pay higher costs as a consequence of fraud in sports, and the 'quality' of sport may suffer indirectly as a result of corruption. Many consumer frauds take place at recreational facilities, such as overcharging for beverages at large-scale gatherings when it is expected that people will be less watchful.

Companies are now involved in a considerably broader spectrum of crimes than previously thought. Price fixing, stock market manipulation, insider trading, anticompetitive market manipulations, the formation of illegal cartels, the manufacture

---

[86] Frank Pearce & Steve Tombs, *Toxic Capitalism: Corporate Crime and the Chemical Industry* 16(1st ed. 1988).

[87] S. Kulkarni, *Biomedical Waste Management in India*, 2 Bio Medical Engennering Internatinal,86 (2020).

[88] Gagandeep Singh Dhillon, *Himachal PPE Scam: Health top official sought bribe, never got it, investigators inform court*, The Indian Express (May 29, 2020) https://indianexpress.com/article/india/himachal-ppe-kit-scam-health-official-bribe-6431978/.Jour

of highly dangerous products, employment offences, bribery, tax evasion, industrial espionage, and now even corporate manslaughter[89].

ON PENALIZATION OF CORPORATE OFFENCES

"Unhindered corporate force creates exorbitant social harm."

Since organizations are more powerful than people, it has been determined that organizations can do more prominent damage than people acting individually. Australian criminologist, John Braithwaite simply defines corporate crimes as "The conduct of corporation or of employees acting on behalf of a corporation, which is proscribed and punishable by law."[90] Although corporate offences are not authentically defined anywhere under Indian laws, its elemental structure is derived from Section 11 of Indian Penal Code, 1860 which states that *"the word person includes any Company or Association or a body of persons, whether incorporated or not."[91] Implicating the idea that businesses shall be penalized in the same way as a natural person. Although it is very obscure to understand that how a business (unit) can be imprisoned as a natural person.*

The aforementioned fallacy of Indian jurisprudence on penalization of corporate illegalities was addressed in the judgment of The Assistant Commissioner v. M/S. Velliappa Textiles Ltd. & Anr by Hon' Justice B. N. Srikrishna, he stated that "The first respondent is a company, a juristic person, and therefore, incapable of being punished with a sentence of imprisonment, which is mandatory under the provisions of Sections 276C and 277. Hence, the prosecution under these Sections against a juristic person like a company is not maintainable, even if by reason of Section 278B some other persons connected with it and responsible for running the business of the company can be held liable for the offence."[92] This legal difficulty arising in penalization of corporate offences was also noticed by Law Commission of India and in its 41st report suggestion for amendment of section 62 of IPC was made. The law Commission recommended adding

---

[89] Steve Russell, *From the Red Core to the Black Sky: Corporate Crime in the Transnational Matrix*, Journal Of Criminal Justice And Popular Culture, 148, 155 (2005.)

[90] Sally Simpson, *Corporate Crime, Law And Social Resposibility* 6(1ST ed. 2002)

[91] Indian Penal Code, No.45 of 1860, § 11.

[92] The Assistant Commissioner v. M/S Velliappa Textiles & Anr, (2003) AIR2004SC86(Ind.)

the following lines in section 62 of IPC "In every case in which the offence is only punishable with imprisonment or with imprisonment and fine and the offender is a company or other body corporate or an association of individuals, it shall be competent to the court to sentence such offender to fine only."[93] To clarify this subject a bit more, Law Commission again in its 47th report recommended via paragraph 8 that: In many of the Acts relating to economic offences, imprisonment is mandatory. Where the convicted person is a corporation, this provision becomes unworkable, and it is desirable to provide that in such cases, it shall be competent to the court to impose a fine. This difficulty can arise under the Penal Code also, but it is likely to arise more frequently in the case of economic laws. We, therefore, recommend that the following provision should be inserted in the Penal Code as, say, Section 62:-

"(1) In every case in which the offence is punishable with imprisonment only or with imprisonment and fine, and the offender is a corporation, it shall be competent to the court to sentence such offender to fine only.

(2) In every case in which the offence is punishable with imprisonment and any other punishment not being fined, and the offender is a corporation, it shall be competent to the court to sentence such offender to fine.

(3) In this section, 'corporation' means an incorporated company or other body corporate, and includes a firm and other association of individuals."[94]

Relying on these recommendations by Law Commission of India Supreme Court in the landmark judgment of Standard Chartered Bank & Ors v. Directorate of Enforcement & Ors [95] said that there is no blindfold immunity for any organization from the prosecution of offenses in light of the fact that the offence committed requires a mandatory imprisonment. The apex court hereby concluded that in instances of offenses which command both detainment and fine, the corporate shall be liable for the payment of fine only. This historic judgment set the precedent for all forthcoming cases against

---

[93] law commission of India, gov't of Ind. 41st reporT,191(1969), https://lawcommissionofindia.nic.in/1-50/Report41.pdf

[94] law commission of India, gov't of Ind. 47th report,62(1972), https://lawcommissionofindia.nic.in/1-50/Report47.pdf

[95] Standard Charted Bank & Ors v. Directorate of Enforcement & Ors,(2005) 4 SCC 530 (Ind.)

corporate crimes in India, until recently in 2019 when Ministry Of Corporate Affairs decriminalized 16 out of 81 compoundable offences listed under Companies Act, 2013[96] through the Companies (amendment) Act, 2020. To further decriminalize Company offences following changes were also made under Companies (amendment) Act, 2020:-

- 23 offences that related to minor illegalities were re-categorized from criminal offences to issues that can be resolved by In-House Adjudication Mechanism.
- 7 offences were omitted from the Companies Act as they were better dealt by other provisions of law.
- 11 offences that have subjective determination and are not of very grievous nature may contain the penalty of just offence rationalized fine.

Even though these latest amendments in Companies Act, 2013 decriminalized most of the offences listed under the act. Offences which are non-compoundable and grave in nature still attract criminal liability.

The issue of criminalization of illegal acts of corporations has always been of controversial nature and with ever evolving status of Indian jurisprudence; corporate criminal liability has always attracted conflict of opinions among legal fraternity. Enforcement of Companies (amendment) Act, 2020 by Government of India has again ignited a spark in the contemporary debate that should a company be penalized under criminal laws of India or should its offences be treated as civil breaches of law as company is not a real person and it cannot be imprisoned.

Authors further in paper discuss pros and cons of decriminalization of corporate offences.

Arguments in favor of decriminalization of corporate offences:-

- **Easing the workload of Indian Judicial Forum**

Disproportionate ratio between numbers of cases per court has left Indian justice system overwhelmed with plethora of pending cases. According to data collected by National Judicial Data Grid (NJDG) in June, 2021 a ginormous total of 2, 85, 23,812

[96] Ministry of Corporate affairs, gov't of Ind., report of the committee to review offences under the companies act, 2013, 5 (2018), https://www.mca.gov.in/Ministry/pdf/ReportCommittee_28082018.pdf

[97]criminal cases still remain pending before Indian courts. To lighten the burden on judicial forums and to ensure speedy trials to corporate, Companies (amendment) Act, 2020 under section 454 introduced In-house Adjudication Mechanism (IAM)[98].

According to the IAM Framework, a mediating official ("AO") is giver authority to settle offenses by charging the applicable penalty from the defaulting organizations and additionally from officials' in-default. Orders of the AO are appealable to the local chief ("RD") of the MCA. NON- compliance of such orders (of the AO or the RD) draws in criminal consequences. As a compelling obstruction, rehashed defaults within a period of 3 (three) years from the date of settlement under the IAM Framework attract higher penalty.

Legislative introduction of IAM has reduced the burden on special courts such as NCLT by eliminating minor and technical offences such as non-maintenance of registers[99], etc from their jurisdiction. This framework also provides cost and time effective disposal of cases as opposed to traditional prosecution method.

- **Civil prosecution of company offences would be more proficient.**

A few professionals contend for corporate criminal offenses to be totally replaced by civil prosecution as criminal trials are complex and time consuming and it is very strenuous to establish corporate criminal liability. Essential pre conditions for a criminal trial are presence of mens rea i.e. guilty mind and actus reus i.e. the wrongful act. As for manifesting corporate criminal liability prosecutors and the authorities struggle to demonstrate mens rea of a non-natural person, a company. Therefore imposition of a civil suit for procedural defaults of a company benefits organizations as well as the controllers, since it would eliminate the necessity of demonstrating mens rea which is a precondition in criminal trials. In Director of Enforcement v. MCTM Corporation [100] Supreme Court held that civil liability is imposed for 'blameworthy conduct' and that guilty intention is not a *sine qua non*. In addition, the threshold for burden of proof is

---

[97] https://njdg.ecourts.gov.in/njdgnew/index.php

[98] The Companies (Amendment) Act, No. 29 of 2020, §454 (Ind.)

[99] The Companies Act, No. 18 of 2013, §88(5) (Ind.).

[100] Director of Enforcement v. MCTM Corporation Pvt. Ltd, (1996) 2 SCC 471, (Ind.).

higher for criminal offences, which must be proved 'beyond all reasonable doubt' whereas it is sufficient to establish 'preponderance of probability' for imposing civil liability.

- **Ease of doing business**

The main raison d'être of government behind decriminalization of offences under company law is to attract foreign investments and promote small businesses growth through relaxed and liberalized business laws. The ambiguity and tediousness of lengthy court procedure required for doing business in India has been a major discouragement for foreign investors establishing business in India. The agitation of attracting criminal ramifications for minor and frivolous matters among the business owners additionally go against the policy of ease of doing business. Decriminalization of such matters will fundamentally urge business owners and probable investors to undertake business ventures in the nation, without dreading of any criminal consequences.

<u>Arguments against decriminalization of corporate offences:-</u>

- **Scrapping of criminal sanctions may increase corruption.**

The existence of stringent penal provisions keep corporate sector of the nation in check. Decriminalization of company wrongs and replacing rigor punishments with mere fine may adversely affect corporate responsibility towards state and public. It could likewise trigger intentional infringement of law with the agreement that the punishment forced would be significantly less than the benefit acquired from the law breaking.

- **Fixed penalties are prejudiced towards businesses with huge turnover.**

India is a land of diverse businesses with different turnovers, ranging from rupees fifty thousand to fifty thousand crores and imposition of a fixed penalty on companies of varying sizes is restrictive and arbitrary in nature. As Supreme Court pointed out in Adamji Umar Dalal v. State of Bombay [101] situations related with the incident of wrongdoing ought to be considered while choosing a specific punishment for a offense. If not, there can be cases with extraordinary conditions, which if not considered would prompt an inordinate punishment being forced, accordingly making colossal damage to

---

[101] Adamji Umar Dalal v. State of Bombay, (1952) SCR 172 (Ind.).

an indivisual. Imposition of fine for commission of crimes is only beneficial if it has repercussions. A company with huge turnover suppose of twenty million may consider payment of rupees 1 lakh as penalty a minimal fee it has to pay for achieving its desired objective. While on the other hand a penalty of 1 lakh may make a company with turnover of rupees 50 thousand bankrupt. Moreover imposition of a fixed penalty may have adverse effect on investors and financers of a company contradicting the basic aim of attracting foreign investors.

ROLE OF CORPORATE GOVERNANCE IN CORPORATE CRIMES

Corporate crimes have an indirect concerning effect on the public, and dealing with cases of corporate crimes in court is also a tedious task as it is confounding to decide how to penalize corporate. As an outcome, the quote "prevention is better than cure" holds relevance over here and how corporate governance should be given high priority in order to prevent corporate crimes.

Corporate governance in a concise way can be defined as a framework for managing and supervising companies.[102] In this sense, corporate governance is a set of processes that allow a corporation to function where ownership and management are separate, it establishes a framework within which the company's goals are set, methods for achieving them are developed, and the owner's oversight of the company's operations is exercised. If the corporate governance structure is sound, it will provide effective incentives to achieve the objectives in the company's and hold shareholders' best interests. This in turn will help to improve the efficiency of operations oversight, which as a consequence will have a direct impact on resource utilisation.

Corporate governance is the way in which the shareholders, directors, management, and suppliers, as well as employees, primary clients engage with one another in a limited liability corporation. Corporate governance principles, both formal and informal, can be found in every nation's legal, institutional, and regulatory structure. Great corporate

---

[102] Committee on the Financial Aspects of Corporate Governance, and Adrian Cadbury. Report of the committee on the financial aspects of corporate governance, 1992, 14 (UK).

governance ought to give legitimate incentives to the Board of Directors and the executives for accomplishing goals that are to the greatest advantage of the firm and its investors, and make management activities simpler and more proficient

Corporate governance is subject to a steady and proficient general set of laws just like an institutional climate that takes into consideration the arrangement of organizations and their suitable activity. In any case, such an atmosphere might be set up by sure turn of events, which will prevent abuse of power, and speculations won't be made until enterprises are sure that the undertaking's danger and the "state's" hazard are both reasonable.

Considering the corporate governance framework, the OECD recommended (1998) to national governments and other relevant international institutions such as the World Bank and the private sector to define corporate governance rules and principles. The principles constitute a broad framework that governments consider essential for the development of good governance practices. They should be concise, comprehensible, and accessible to the international community, and they should concentrate on the following:

1. Establishing a foundation for effective corporate governance
2. Shareholder rights and their involvement
3. Transparency
4. Board responsibility[103]

However weak corporate governance can create frictionless way for corporate crimes. One such paradigm of weak corporate governance can be seen in the case of *'Satyam Scam'*. Satyam scam was India's largest corporate fraud carried out by manipulating the company's income statements, cash flows, and balance sheet for over seven years as admitted by B. Ramalinga Raju, the founder and chairman of Satyam Computer services. Overstated revenues and earnings were part of the $1.47 billion fraud on Satyam's balance sheet, which was conducted by the company's founder and his brother, the CEO, in order to attract more business and avert a hostile takeover. "It was like being on a

[103] Angel Gurria, *G20/Oecd Principles Of Corporate Governance*, 22(2015)

tiger and not knowing how to get off without getting eaten," said Raju in his confession statement[104]. Satyam had been widely praised for exceptional corporate governance, and Raju had been regarded as a role model for successful business and entrepreneurship. The founder and his co-conspirators recorded fraudulent cash deposits, misstatements of accounts receivables and payables, understated liabilities, and exaggerated assets; these deceptions were only exposed when Raju attempted to buy two additional family-owned businesses. Shareholders were outraged by the proposed acquisition because they saw it as an attempt to prop up other struggling family firms by siphoning funds from the thriving software company.

Indian shareholders have already lost more than $2 billion in corporate crimes and weak governance since 2003,[105] even before the Satyam affair broke. Only 4 out of 68 Indian companies were found to adhere to "highly desirable" disclosure standards in a report released on January 7, 2009 by an analyst at one of India's leading investment houses; more than half of the companies on the list that did not make the grade were well-known companies with significant global presence.[106]

In all authors contend that corporate government has a major role to play in a company illegal activities. Ethical governance may keep irregulaties on part of the firm under check while bad corporate governance with rampant opportunist behavior may feloniously affect company activities.

CONCLUSION

Corporate offences and government efforts to curb them are not new in India. What started with liberalization policy in 1991 is being carried forward with CAA, 2020. The motive of government behind all the efforts to decriminalize the offences of corporations is to de clog the justice system and to increase growth of businesses in India. The maxim *"lex non cogit ad imposibilia"* i.e. law does not contemplate which

---

[104] The Economist Group Limited, *India's Enron*, THE ECONOMIST (Jan.8, 2009). https://www.economist.com/business/2009/01/08/indias-enron.

[105] *Corporate India's governance crisis*, Business Week, (Feb.2, 2009).

[106] *Id.*

cannot be done precisely defines the situation of Indian courts on criminal liability of corporate units.

Keeping in view the above stated legal maxim authors of this paper believe that Companies Act (Amendment), 2020 with help of good corporate governance can curtail corporate offences to a great extent.

DRINK AND DRIVE IN CHECKPOST- NAKAS
A DETAILED ANALYSIS OF THE LOOPHOLES IN THE PRESENT LAWS AND ITS CONSEQUENCES.

DR. JAYKUMAR BHONGALE*
MR. OISHIK BHATTACHARYA*

ABSTRACT

As mentioned in a Times of India Report, more than 70% of the road accidents in India is due to drinking and driving. The device used at the drink and drive checkpoints are called Breathalyzers. The legal limit of being drunk while driving in India, as specified by the Transport Ministry is 0.3 % per 100ml blood. This technology mechanically detects the blood alcohol concentration (BAC) by means of two techniques a breath based sensor and touch based sensor. The breath based system will measure the alcohol concentration in the blood through the driver's exhaled air. Touch based sensor will read the alcohol level below the skin surface. We will be dealing with the breath based sensors in this paper. Here, we will be discussing about the unhyegenic factors of a breath based alcohol test. The probable diseases that can be spread by the continuous use of the said device. If there are any laws in India governing the checkpoints? Comparison of the drunk and drive implications in India with that of the other common law countries like United Kingdom, Canada, and Australia. This paper also introduces measures to secure the use of same. What are the probable bars on using an alcohol breath tester during the widespread of the global pandemic - Covid 19?

INTRODUCTION

It has been known that alcohol use impairs driving skills and increases accident risk. It has been found that while driving under the influence of alcohol, the risk of having an accident causing injury or death increases exponentially. Drunk driving has a high

* Assistant Professor, Bharati Vidyapeeth Deemed to be University, New Law College Pune.
* Student of BBA LLB SEM VII, Bharati Vidyapeeth Deemed to be University, New Law College Pune.

probability to lead to serious accidents. Even with a small amount of alcohol assumption, drivers are twice likely to be involved in traffic accidents than sober drivers. Therefore, many countries have been working on solutions to drunk driving for a long period of time, including publicity and education and tough drunk-driving laws. The laws have been enacted to prohibit driving after drinking and have imposed severe penalties on violators. The legal limits for BAC are between 0.01% and 0.08%. The limit, for example, is 0.02% in Sweden; 0.05% in Israel, Korea, and Australia; and 0.08% in Canada, England, Mexico, and the United States. In China, driving with a BAC higher than 0.02% is defined as drink-driving and the driver will be penalized. Moreover, driving with a BAC higher than 0.08% is considered drunken-driving and it belongs to unlawful act.

Even so, drinking driving is still difficult to be completely eliminated. It is also needed to analyze the signatures of alcohol's impairment on drivers to pave the foundation for the study on the countermeasure of drinking driving. Alcohol can affect drivers' cognition, vigilance, attention, judgment, and reaction, which were related to driving ability closely. It was concluded that alcohol consumption, even at low doses, significantly affected driving-related skills such as vision, braking behaviour, and vigilance. At the same time, drivers' information process and attention were heavily affected by alcohol. Nash demonstrated that drivers would be distracted by alcohol when they were asked to complete some tasks. It has been indicated that alcohol would negatively affect drivers' ability on judgment of following distance and depth perception. Alcohol's effects on visual performance are most obvious when it comes to the judgment of moving objects and the process of different information at the same time found that alcohol affected many parameters for a long time, including simple reaction times, vigilance, visual searches, and logical reasoning.

According to research 13000 people are killed from alcohol impaired driving. To be more focused the statistics comes to 35 people per day. To curb this statistics down educational institutions should convey messages to their students on the consequences drunk driving because teenagers are more likely to get into a car crash which leads to death. Teachers must imbibe the thoughts about the legal ramification which will consecutives lead to fall of drunk driving. If the teens get to know about the death rate and he peer pressure then it will decrease the fatal car crashes.

Study says that teenagers in India are 17 times more likely to involve in fatal car crashes than any sober driver.

SCOPE

Different- different strategies are used by police officials to keep a check on drunken drivers. Usually police from local stations set up road blocks on the roads forcing passing vehicles to slow down and pass the roadblock in a one to one pattern enabling police officials to stop each vehicle to test for the alcohol levels.

CHECK-POSTS/ ROAD BLOCKS

Police check-post also called "Nakas" are set up on the road to check drunk and driving or DUI or DWI (Driving while intoxicated). The idea and motive behind setting up of check-posts is to keep in check the offenders so that public safety as well as public order is maintained. However a question of harassment is raised for the people who aren't offenders or the people who didn't break any rules. For instance, in the scenario of drink and drive barricades/ check post, there usually is checking of each and every vehicle and moreover the passage is narrow which leads up long queues and traffic jams resulting in inconvenience for people. Moreover rather than becoming a check on offenders it becomes a hurdle in emergency situations like for Ambulances etc.

BREATHALYSER

To test breath alcohol content police official use a device called "**breathalyzer**".

It gives an estimate of alcohol content in the blood stream of the person. To check the person has to breathe into the device, Then after the breathe air has circulated in the device, the alcohol level gets picked up by the device, by detection of alcohol molecules present in the breathe which has come from lungs

A breathalyser estimates an individual's blood alcohol levels. When a person breathes into the device, it picks up on the molecular content of alcohol in the breath from the lungs and converts it into the approximate blood alcohol level.

India doesn't have a proper framework or set standards for the use of equipment's like breathalysers. It doesn't have proper framework to comply with in case of the Breathalyzer or even for its use. There are no set standards for technology as well as the basic requirement pertaining to the mechanical structure to be termed as breath alcohol analyser.

Breath analyzer/alcohol meter falls within the definition of "weight or measure" as it is used to measure the Blood Alcohol Content (BAC) and hence, specification and calibration is required to be done as per the provisions of the Legal Metrology Act of 2009 and the supporting rules. Breath analyzers vary from one to another. And they are built in a way which requires calibration after certain period of time to make it work again or it plays defect information. Some are to be necessarily calibrated every six months. In Dharmendra Yashovardhan vs State N.C.T. Of Delhi & Anr[107], court stated that if nothing has been put forward to validate the requirement of calibration every six months, the same, be taken as twelve months as per the Legal Metrology Rules. Thus it cannot be denied that it is important to calibrate the breath analyzer periodically to maintain accuracy and reliability of the test.

Breathalyzers also gets defeated on the purpose of checking people driving under the influence as it only checks drunk and driving but not who are driving under the influence of substance abuse like who are under the influence of narcotics. Since just like alcohol abuse, narcotics or use of drugs also impair the basic decision making power of the body and making driving dangerous.

LAWS GOVERNING DRINKING AND DRIVING IN INDIA

I. [108]ROAD TRANSPORT AND SAFETY BILL, 2015

Under Chapter I - Section 3 (13) of this act, the term "driver" is defined as any person who drives or steers a motor vehicle.

---

[107] MANU/DEOR/209420/2022.

[108]Road Transprt and Safety Bill, 2015 available online at http://www.indiaenvironmentportal.org.in/files/file/ROAD%20TRANSPORT%20AND%20SAFETY%20BILL%202015.pdf

Section (300) of Chapter XIV - Offences and Penalties - **Driving under the influence of alcohol or drugs:**

1. A person shall be punishable in accordance with sub-section (2) if, while driving, or attempting to drive a motor vehicle, such person is deemed to have alcohol in his breath or blood on an impairment test, on a test by a breath analyser, or any other test including clinical test.

2. The punishment for driving, or attempting to drive, a motor vehicle under sub-section (1) shall be, in addition to the awarding of penalty points in accordance with Schedule II, punishable in accordance with Schedule III.

3. A person who, while driving, or attempting to drive a motor vehicle, is under the influence of a narcotic, or a psychotropic substance or a drug or a prescription drug as prescribed by the Central Government in this behalf, by notification, shall be punishable in accordance with Schedule III, if:

(a) the person does not complete a compulsory impairment test in a manner satisfactory to a police officer under section (324), provided that any such police officer should be trained to give such test in the manner specified by the National Authority; and

(b) the person's blood or urine, as ascertained from an analysis through a clinical test subsequently taken under section (327) contains evidence of the use of a drug or drugs as specified by the National Authority.

4. A police officer may arrest a person without warrant if the person refuses or fails to comply with provisions of sections (326) and (327).

5. Any driver of a motor vehicle, carrying a child or children in the vehicle, who violates sub-section (1) or sub-section (3) of this section, shall be punishable in accordance with Schedule III, and subjected to an immediate cancellation of license for a period of three years.

6. Any person who drives a transport vehicle or aheavy motor vehicle and violates sub-section (1) or sub-section (3) of this section shall be punishable in accordance with Schedule III, and subjected to an immediate cancellation of license for a period of five years.

7. Any person who has committed an offense under sub-section (3) of this section will have a valid defence, if the court is satisfied that the person had consumed the relevant qualifying drug: (a) in accordance with: (i) a current and valid prescription written for that person by a registered medical practitioner; and 270 (ii) any instructions from a registered medical practitioner or from the manufacturer of the qualifying drug; or a. because it was administered by a registered medical practitioner, provided that the person complied with the instructions (if any) that the registered medical practitioner has given.

8. It is no defence to proceedings for an offense that a provision forming part of sections (324), (326) and (327) has not been strictly complied with or has not been complied with at all, provided there has been reasonable compliance with such of those provisions as apply.

II. MOTOR VEHICLES ACT,1988

Section 185 of the Motor Vehicles Act, 1988 depicts the punishment to be handed down to motor vehicle drivers who are found to have consumed more alcohol than the prescribed limit. No action are often taken against a driver whose blood alcohol content (BAC) is less than this limit. However, if the blood alcohol content is found to be greater than 30 mg, he are often imprisoned for a period which can extend up to six months or a fine not exceeding Rs. 2,000 or both for the first offence. If the same offence is repeated within a period of 3 years, the offender can be imprisoned for a term not exceeding 2 years or asked to pay a fine not exceeding Rs. 3,000 or both.

THE AMENDMENT –

From 1st September 2019, the fines for road safety have been increased heavily. The fine for a **drink and drive** under the Motor Vehicle (Amendment) Bill 2016 has been risen from 2000/- to 10,000/-

In the case of drunken driving, these are the new amended fines:

- For the first offence, there is imprisonment up to a period of 6 months and/or a penalty of INR 10,000, which has gone up from the erstwhile fine of INR 2,000

However, for the second offence, the imprisonment clause is 2 years and/or a penalty of INR 15,000, which has gone up from the erstwhile fine of INR 3,000/- Section 203 of the MV Act deals with Breath Tests. The relevant portion for our purpose is given below:

"**203**. Breath tests.-(1) A police officer in uniform or an officer of the Motor Vehicles Department, as may be authorized in this behalf by that Department, may require any person driving or attempting to drive a automobile during a public place to supply one or more specimens of breath for breathtest there or nearby, if such policeman or officer has any reasonable cause to suspect him of getting committed an offence under section 185:

If a person, required by a police officer under sub-section (1) or sub-section (2) to provide a specimen of breath for a breath test, refuses or fails to do so and the policeman has reasonable cause to suspect him of getting alcohol in his blood, the policeman may arrest him without warrant except while he's at a hospital as an indoor patient.

III.SECTION 279 OF INDIAN PENAL CODE

Rash driving or riding on a public way.—Whoever drives any vehicle, or rides, on any public way in a manner so rash or negligent as to endanger human life, or to be likely to cause hurt or injury to any other person, shall be punished with imprisonment of either description for a term which may extend to six months, or with fine which may extend to one thousand rupees, or with both.

ROAD ISSUES IN INDIA

A study on drivers killed in road crashes has revealed that teenage drivers have quite 5 times the danger of a crash compared with drivers aged 30 and above, at all level of BAC. A Road Accident Statistics in India showed by the NDTV gives a rough age of drivers who face road accident. 22 to 29 years old males were estimated to possess 3 times the danger compared with drivers aged 30 years and above, in the least BAC levels. Alcohol consumption by drivers puts pedestrians and riders of motorized two wheelers in danger.

In Sanjeev Nanda v The State Case[109] discussed below the Hon'ble Court highlights an equivalent well. In the case, State Transport Police Station Lodhi Road vs. Sanjeev Nanda[110] important judgment from perspective of road safety emerged. The Respondent during this case was charged under Section 201[111], 304 (I)[112], 308[113] r/w section 34[114] IPC for driving his car rashly and negligently and hitting 7 persons. It was further observed by court that it's different.

PROCEDURE

In India, highway safety laws of all kinds are generally enforced by fixed sobriety checkpoints manned by personnel from the local police station. Barriers are arranged on the roadway so that passing vehicles are forced to slow down, and the officers on duty signal selected vehicles to pull over as they pass through the barriers. If the roadblock is intended to target drunken driving, police personnel then ask the driver a few questions on his or her identity, destination, etc., while observing the driver's demeanor and smelling his or her breath. If the police feel the driver may be drunk, then according to the official procedure they will order him or her to blow into the breathalyzer, following the results of which the driver is either charged or released. The printed results of a handheld breathalyzer are considered sufficient proof of drunkenness in court.

Once caught, drunken drivers' vehicles are confiscated by the police, and the driver must appear in court to pay a fine or potentially face jail time, although imprisonment is never observed in our data. The fine amount depends largely on the judgment of the local magistrate, with a maximum fine of Rs. 2000 4 (roughly $50) for the first offence 1. The driver must then return to the police station to recover the vehicle from the police lot.

---

109 Sanjeev Nanda v The State, (2012) 8 SCC 450.
110 Sanjeev Nanda v The State, (2012) 8 SCC 450.
111 Causing disappearance of Evidence of Offence, or giving False Information to Screen Offenders.
112 Punishment for Culpable Homicide not Amount to Murder.
113 Attempt To Commit Culpable Homicide.
114 Section 34 Indian penal Code

Even this official procedure leaves many factors undetermined and up to the discretion of the police manning the roadblock. The choice of how many, and which, vehicles to pull over for questioning and potential testing is the most important. Ideally the police should target vehicles with the highest probability of drunkenness, and in conversations the police often noted that if they saw a vehicle with a family, or driven by elderly people they assumed that the driver would be unlikely to be drunk and let it pass. Other considerations may also enter the decision: police may be less likely to stop vehicles with many passengers who would be difficult to deal with at an isolated police station if the vehicle were impounded. Similarly, the police might be hesitant to stop luxury vehicles whose owners might be well connected and cause problems if subjected to breath testing.

Unscrupulous police officers are faced with another decision: whether to follow the official ticketing procedure or instead to solicit (or accept) a bribe from the accused drunken driver. There are several stages in the encounter when this exchange could take place. Police may either demand (or take) a side payment prior to the breathalyzer test, if it is clear the driver is drunk, or only after the driver has proven his or her drunkenness via the official test. Corruption may also occur that the final stage when once-drunken drivers return to the police station to recover their impounded vehicles, when police may demand excess payments to release the vehicles.

STATEMENT OF PROBLEMS

The topic drunk driving plays a vital role in the Indian legal structure consisting of a lot of loopholes in it.

SECTION 279

The Act (Sec 279) may be called the IPC (Amendment) Act, 2007.The section deals with rash and negligent driving thus giving a imprisonment of a six months of imprisonment or a fine of Rs 1000 or both.

When a vehicle mows down a person, the police starts the case with sec 279 of IPC and 304A, which pertains to rash and negligent driving causing death due to same. Although the offences are bailable within some certain hours of accident. Recently ,the Supreme court while considering the increasing number of vehicular accidents resulting in death of large number of innocent people has favoured the punishment under 304A for two years is grossly inadequate.

Therefore, it is high time that amendment be made in sec 279 and 304A of IPC by prescribing stringent punishment besides making offence under 304A.thus it cannot be said as a good deterrence.

It is horrible but true not a single day goes without a report in the newspaper about a mother or school child or a poor man crushed by a bus or some vehicle. Rash and negligent driving causes more than 60,000 deaths per year. The incident of drunken driving in the urban areas are rising menacingly. Drunken bus drivers and youngsters with the steering in their hand acts insane on road, as if there are no laws to check them rightly so in view of weak provision of law which hardly act as a deterrent and the present position of law does not act as deterrent for the offenders. Thus it is high time to amend the sec 185 of the MV Act.

SECTION 295

Section 295A in the Indian Penal Code

Deliberate and malicious acts, intended to outrage reli-gious feelings of any class by insulting its religion or reli-gious beliefs.—Whoever, with deliberate and malicious intention of outraging the religious feelings of any class of 273 [citizens of India], 274 [by words, either spoken or written, or by signs or by visible representations or otherwise], insults or attempts to insult the religion or the religious beliefs of that class, shall be punished with imprisonment of either description for a term which may extend to 4[three years], or with fine, or with both.]

In a pronouncement that reiterates the constitutional protection to freedom of speech and expression, the Supreme Court has said that unwitting or careless "insults" to religion should not be prosecuted as this would amount to misuse of law.

Concerned by the misuse of Section 295A of IPC, which provides up to three years' jail term for hurting religious sentiments, the Supreme Court limited the applicability of the penal provision to deliberate and malicious acts rather than casual observations that are not driven by malicious intent.

It is clear as crystal that Section 295A does not stipulate everything to be penalised and any and every act would tantamount to insult or attempt to insult the religion or the religious beliefs of class of citizens. It penalises only those acts of insults or those varieties of attempts to insult the religion or religious belief of a class of citizens which are perpetrated with the deliberate and malicious intention of outraging the religious feelings.

BREATH ANALYZER RESULT DISCREPENCY

Breathalyzers have had a long history of controversy over their effectiveness and validity when used as evidence in a court of law.

Breath Testing has become a tool frequently used by police officers throughout India.

1. Just how accurate are these machines?

2. How important are they to a prosecutor in a prosecution for operating a motor vehicle, or other motorized device, under the influence of alcohol (DWI/DUI)?

3. Where can their reliability as accurate predictors of true blood alcohol content be attacked?

Where does breath testing fit within a DWI/DUI investigation? The breath test is relied upon by jurors as the God of evidence. Most citizens believe if an officer received a reading of 30mg or greater from his administered breath test the defendant was surely impaired by alcohol. A result of 30mg or more may be a legal inference but the publicity has done its job, you're guilty now prove you're not guilty. Many jurors upon hearing the Breath Alcohol Content (BAC) is 30mg or greater, at the beginning of trial, conclude improperly that the case is over and the defendant has lost his case As will be seen below, reliance by the general public is seriously misplaced and the validity of this blind conclusion cannot be justified.

To properly address breath testing and how it fits within the framework of a DUI investigation the reliance upon field sobriety testing must also be briefly considered because what is observed by an officer must by definition fit the picture of impairment.

Field sobriety testing is completely subjective. A trained officer is looking for errors within a myriad of possibilities while the test taker is performing as well as is possible under the rigors of a stressful and fearful event, performing foreign tests described and demonstrated by less than perfect biased test giver. The giver is only interested in the errors he has been trained to focus upon while the performer only cares about how well he can perform. (Many of the questions asked by officers before any testing are designed to discover unique problems that may affect a person's performance on the pending test. The degree to which an officer considers the answers he receives from his subject is variable to each officer) The true performance is not always reported, The same can be said of breath testing results.

Are Breathalyzers A Violation Of Civil Rights?

The uses of breathalyzers are becoming increasingly popular among police officers in India. In recent years, more and more people are going to jail due to a breathalyzer result. The question is whether or not breathalyzers are even entirely accurate. If they aren't, can the truly be admissible in court? For example, let's say a college student of drinking age meets up with a friend for dinner. The student shares a small pitcher of margaritas with her friend over the course of three hours.

When she decides to head home, she is stopped by a DUI checkpoint. The police officer who stops her claims he saw her car swerve into another lane. Unfortunately, the officer can legally lie to her and say he saw her swerving, even if he didn't. He then administers a breathalyzer after asking how much she had to drink. Being the honest student she is, she tells the officer she had two margaritas. Although her BAC was below the legal limit of 30mg, she is still arrested for possibly being above the limit. This particular student is attending college on a scholarship and is now facing possible termination of said scholarship after word of her arrest gets out.

Believe it or not, this exact scenario occurs more often than you might think. Even being arrested for suspected drunk driving can ruin any chances of a perfect record. One faulty breathalyzer test can interfere with future scholarships or other important life events. So why are breathalyzers still a way of testing how intoxicated a person is? According to the Centers for Disease Control, more than 30 percent of vehicle-related deaths occur every year due to drunk drivers. Breathalyzers are routinely administered by police officers to ensure impaired drivers stay off the road. There is, however, a growing concern that the most significant tool utilized to identify drunk drivers is flawed. As a result, breathalyzers could possibly violate a driver's civil rights.

The Issue of Implied Consent

In the majority of cases, police do give drivers an option, depending on a state law called implied consent. But some states, punish drivers who refuse to take alcohol tests. Drivers can either take the test or risk the same jail time as a DUI conviction, suspension of their license and/or a major fine. According to the NHTSA, 22 percent of suspected drunk drivers refused breath tests in 2015.

Since then, refusal rates have dropped in 11 states and increased in 12 others, with refusals averaging between 19 and 25 percent.

Is the Legal Limit a Concrete Number?

Breath tests are used to assess whether a driver has too much alcohol in his or her system, but as we know, that level varies from state to state. States now all use a .08 percent blood alcohol content reading as the legal intoxication limit, but there have been cases where drivers are arrested for blowing much lower than the legal limit. There is even a push to lower the limit to .05, a number causing much controversy.

This is an issue in itself regarding civil rights because it essentially suggests people not drink while they are out. Fifty to 75 percent of convicted drunk drivers, however, decide to drive again even after their license has been suspended, cites Mothers Against Drunk Driving (MADD). It is also expressed that drivers have been intoxicated behind the wheel at least 80 times before they are arrested for the first time. This could be fuel for a lower legal limit. The push for this new limit is still in its infancy, of course, so there is no need to follow this "new" rule right now.

RECOMMENDATION

There should be an anti-driving programme which should follow a straightforward randomized control trial (RCT) setup, consisting of three overlapping experiments, each varying a different aspect of how the campaign was implemented:

1) The frequency of the roadblocks. Roadblocks should be carried out in the police station jurisdiction either 1, 2, or 3 nights per week.

2) The personnel carrying out the roadblock. Roadblocks should be staffed by either, a. Police officers from the local police station (the status quo outside the intervention). b. A dedicated team selected from the police reserve force at the district level. These special teams will monitor by GPS devices installed in their vehicles.

3) The location of the roadblocks. Roadblocks occurred at either,

a. The same spot on every occasion, selected by the local chief of police as the location best suited to preventing accidents due to drunken driving.

b. One of a group of three locations, with each night's location chosen at random. The three spots were chosen by the chief of police as the best three suited to catching drunken drivers.

Roadblock locations

There is a common although certainly not universal hypothesis within the Police and the antidrunken driving literature that surprise checkpoints are more effective than fixed checkpoints always held at the same location and time. To test this hypothesis, and the implicit assumptions of learning by potential and actual drunken drivers, randomly assigned police stations to hold their checkpoints at either a single location, or a rotating set of three locations. In the single location group, the police station chief identifies the best location in the station's jurisdiction for catching drunken drivers, and the checkpoints should be carried out by either local staff or dedicated police lines teams at that location.

Roadblock frequency and timing

The variation in roadblock frequency was designed to identify the shape of the relationship between police enforcement and criminal behavior. In particular, to determine whether this relationship is concave or convex requires at least three points of variation. Discussions with the police determined that it was not feasible to carry out more than 3 roadblocks per week per police station, thus giving us the final randomization categories of 1, 2, or 3 roadblocks per week (and, of course, 0 in the control group). These frequencies were at the police station level, not the road level; for example in a surprise group police station with a frequency of 2 checkpoints per week each of the three roads would have a roadblock twice every three weeks. Checkpoints were always held at 7:00pm-10:00pm in the evening.

Technology to detect driver alcohol content by car

Since 2008, a government-funded research and development program has been designing a universal ignition interlock for all vehicles to prevent drunken driving. The built-in device would measure a driver's blood alcohol level (BAC) to determine whether the person can legally operate a motor vehicle. If not, it would effectively take away the keys by preventing the vehicle from starting.

Such devices are already in widespread use for those charged or convicted of drunken driving. What's different — perhaps even revolutionary — is that the built-in ignition interlock would make an instantaneous and precise reading of every driver's BAC level when the driver attempts to start the vehicle. Eventually, the device could become standard equipment, just like air bags.

The device would take BAC samples in one of two ways. A breath-based system would gather a whiff of a driver's ambient breath. A touch-based system would analyze the touch of a driver's finger, perhaps from a vehicle's starter button or the steering wheel. To win over consumers — and avoid the sort of outcry that occurred in the 1970s over an ill-fated ignition interlock intended to promote seat belt use — project officials say the built-in interlock has to be fast, precise and just about perfectly reliable in many different driving conditions. It also has to have safeguards against drivers who might cheat.

Section 202 of the MV Act, which gives a police officer in uniform to arrest a person in connection to violation of section 185 MV Act talks about the immediate arrest of the person who is found suspicious of drunk driving. However, section 185 and section 203 of the MV Act make it imperative that a person can only be arrested if they have been tested for the amount of alcohol present in their body. The logical inconsistency that the author is trying to point at is that section 202 allows for testing under section 203 after the arrest, whereas, section 203 emphasizes on the point that no arrest can happen without a breath test.

Although, the proviso to section 202 specifies that a person can be tested under section 203 or 204 MV Act within two hours of the arrest but that will be logically inconsistent with sections 185,203,204. The main point that arises here is on what basis the arrest shall be held. MV Act talks about "reasonable suspicion" created in the mind of the officer in charge at the crime scene. The problem with a vaguely phrased term such as that is that different people have different tolerance level.[115] People with high tolerance for alcohol might not appear suspicious but if they are brought to take a breath test, their alcohol level might be well above the permissible limit. Hence, the statute needs to be amended to get rid of the discrepancy.

Another problem with the limit imposed is that some since people have varying tolerance level for alcohol, in some, even a small amount can make them lose complete control of their sense. Someone who is a light weight can be in complete absence of his senses but might only have 15 mg per 100 ml blood alcohol level. Thus, the author advocates for a complete ban on drinking and driving. [116]The effect alcohol has on people depend on a multitude of factors. The weight of a person, prior experience of a person , genetics, amount of food taken before drinking; all these play a vital role in

---

[115] K. Shanmugam v. V. Krishnamurthy and Ors. MANU/TN/7713/2019.

[116] *Ibid.*

determining how drunk a person might get.[117] The setting up of this limit of 30mg alcohol per 100 ml of blood is purely fictional with no factual backing. If this is not possible, then the least that could be done is increasing the limit for professional drivers.

The MV Act nowhere prescribes any rules as to how the breath test or the lab test are to be conducted. The lack of procedural guidelines leads to inconsistencies across regions and adoption of unhygienic methods. There is an absence of a time limit within which results from lab tests are to be given to the accused. This paves way for delays and tampering with evidence. Hence, the need of the hour is to incorporate such laws for a uniform practice to be followed.

In order to encourage the police officers to take their jobs seriously and reduce the chances of accepting bribes, police officers on duty at sobriety checkpoints should be paid extra.[118] Moreover, there needs to be better co-ordination between the License Authority and Officers maintaining the database of drinking and driving offenders. This is to ensure that the license of the offenders are suspended on time.

The state motor vehicle department of every state needs to have a list of alcometers or breath analysers that it distributes in the state. The devices need to be checked and serviced frequently to make sure that they give accurate readings. There needs to be a proper database for the cases registered under section 185 of MV Act. Proper lights on the streets and better maintenance of roads so as to reduce occurrence of any kind of accidents.

Improvement in the methods of investigation so as to make it more scientific. To introduce and implement the system of Native Citizen Cards to maintain complete data of citizens as the country which will facilitate checking of persons and their records.[119] Installation of CCTV cameras on major roads Random checking by the police to prevent the menace of drunken driving specially near pubs, five star hostels, discos etc.

---

[117]Criminal Law Review, The North Review of drink-driving: some sobering proposal, Sally Cunningham, 2011.

[118]JAMES C. FELL , JOHN H. LACEY & ROBERT B. VOAS (2004) Sobriety Checkpoints: Evidence of Effectiveness Is Strong, but Use Is Limited, Traffic Injury Prevention

[119] Sanjeev Nanda v. The State, (2012) 8 SCC 450.

CASES

This section of the paper will deal with cases that have been decided upon by various high courts and the Supreme Court of the country related to drinking and driving. Alcohol, being a neurological depressant, lowers the functioning of the brain.[120]It reaches the nervous system and adsorbs into the body after mixing with the blood stream. Ideally, in order to check the level up to which alcohol has affected the body, one should diagnose the functioning of the brain.[121] However, the same is not possible or practical. Hence, an alternative was evolved which allowed alcohol content in the blood to be checked. The determination of alcohol content in blood closely resembles the level up to which it has affected the nervous system.[122]

The offence of drinking and driving is a cognizable offence.[123] One comes to this conclusion after a conjoint reading of section 2(c) CrPC, section 41 CrPC and section 185, 202 MV Act. Section 185 of MV Act states that any person, when driving a motor vehicle has alcohol in their blood above the limit of 30 mg per 100 ml, that person shall be held liable for the offence of drinking and driving.[124] This testing of the alcohol level in the blood is done through blood test[125] or lab test[126] by the officer in uniform present at the time of offence.

It is often seen that sections of the MV Act are clubbed with IPC provisions. This is solely done because sections 183 to 188 of the MV Act which deal with penalties for drunken or dangerous driving, are silent on the outcome of the accidents.[127] For instance, the MV Act is not sufficient in itself to punish a person who killed someone in the drunken state while driving his vehicle. This is because the maximum punishment that can be given to

---

[120]S. A. Grant, K. Millar, G. N. C. Kenny, Blood alcohol concentration and psychomotor effects, *BJA: British Journal of Anaesthesia*, Volume 85, Issue 3, 1 September 2000, Pages 401–406

[121] https://www.thelancet.com/journals/lanpub/article/PIIS2468-2667(17)30003-8/fulltext

[122]State Tr. P.S. Lodhi Colony New Delhi v. Sanjeev Nanda (03.08.2012 - SC) : MANU/SC/0621/2012.

[123] Rani Shashank Doshi v State of Maharashtra.

[124] Section 185, MV Act.

[125] Section 203, MV Act.

[126] Section, 204, MV Act.

[127] The State of Arunachal Pradesh and Ors. vs. Ramchandra Rabidas and Ors. (04.10.2019 - SC) : MANU/SC/1383/2019.

a person caught under the said section is 3 years. This will defeat the purpose of law and murderers would use this loophole to kill people in a drunken state. The court's reasoning behind such a stance was that both the statutes work independently in their own spheres and cannot be said to lead to incompatible offences.

Drinking and driving is a criminal offence. Hence, the principle of proportionality between crime and punishment[128] becomes of utmost importance in even drunken driving. The MV Act differentiates between first offenders and subsequent offenders. The idea behind doing was perhaps to treat first offenders with leniency. However, this has led to violation of the statutes not being taken seriously. Moreover, the discrepancy between the punishment imposed on first time offenders under both IPC and MV Act is stark.The punishment imposed under the IPC is stricter and more proportionate to the offences relating to motor vehicle accidents in comparison to the MV Act.[129]

The simultaneous application of IPC and MV Act makes one question whether it defeats the purpose of section 26 of General Clauses Act. Section 26 of the General Clauses Act, 1897 provides, "Where an act or omission constitutes an offence under two or more enactments, then the offender shall be liable to be prosecuted and punished under either or any of those enactments, but shall not be liable to be punished twice for the same offence." However, concurrent application of IPC and MV Act shall not be considered a violation of section 26 of general clauses act. It only prohibits the punishment of an offender twice for the same offence but does not bar the trial and or conviction of the offender under both or either enactments.[130]

Courts have often resorted to letting an offender off under the Probation of Offender Act (POA), 1958. The researcher, however, questions the legitimacy and objective of such decisions. The reason why laws are not taken seriously in India is because people always manage to find a loophole in it. The decision to let an offender take the benefit of Section 4 of the POA in drunken driving cases only makes the deterrent component

---

[128] Supra at 3; page no. 9.

[129] Supra at 8; page no. 9.

[130]T.S. Baliah v. T.S. Rangachari1969) 3 SCR 65 : AIR 1969 SC 701 : (1969) 72 ITR 787, State of Maharashtra v. Sayyed Hassan Criminal Appeal No. 1195-1207 of 2018, Decided on September 20, 2018.

of punishment lose its potency.[131] A person driving on the road owes it to the others to carry it out with utmost care and cautiousness. Negligence in driving results not only in the breach of that duty but also endangers the lives of others.[132]

Courts have however not been consistent in their decisions to not give probation in drunken driving cases or cases involving section 304-A IPC. In the case of Yudhbir Singh[133], the high court was of the opinion that the offender should be given the benefit of POA considering the mitigating factors. However, this brings us back to the premise that decisions allowing the probation of offenders only leads to people avoiding compliance with the law, thinking that there is always a way to circumvent its violating. Hence, no leniency should be shown.[134] The statute needs to amend itself to incorporate that no probation should be given under section 304-A IPC. The very reason why IPC is clubbed together with MV Act is because MV Act does not have the means to impose severe punishment on people. If in spite of clubbing IPC with MV Act, the offender is set of easily, it will be a miscarriage of justice.[135]

In the case of Nikhil Wagle[136], the Bombay High Court emphasized on the menace that drinking and driving causes. It's one of the main reasons behind road accidents caused by loss of coordination, poor judgment, slowing down of reflexes and distortion of vision because of the alcohol. The equipment used to check the alcohol content in called a breath analyser or alco meter.[137]The question at the back of the mind is if there is a limit or minimum amount of blood which should be withdrawn for a blood test. The court

---

[131]Subhash v state, MANU/OT/0010/2007.
Subhash Chander and Ors. v. State of Haryana and Ors. (20.09.2007 - Other) : MANU/OT/0010/2007

[132]Bonny D'souza v State of Goa MANU/MH/3183/2018.
Bonny D'Souza v. The State of Goa (22.11.2018 - BOMHC) : MANU/MH/3183/2018.

[133] Yudhbir Singh v State of Himachal Pradesh. MANU/SCOR/38909/2019.
Yudhbir Singh and Anr. v. The State of Himachal Pradesh and Ors. (18.10.2019 - SC Order) : MANU/SCOR/38909/2019.

[134] Vinod Kumar v State of Himachal Pradesh,Dalbir Singh versus State of Haryana 2000 (5) SCC 822000 Indlaw SC 255, State of Punjab versus Saurabh Bakshi2015 (5) SCC182 2015 Indlaw SC 223.

[135] Sanjeev Nanda and Ors. V. State 2009 V AD (Delhi) 785 , Rattan Singh v. State of Punjab (1979) 4 SCC 719 , Ram Singh Vs. State of NCT of Delhi, Shri Shanmugasundaram V. State of Maharashtra , Siddharam Satlingappa Mhetre V. State of Maharashtra and Ors, (2011) 1 SCC 694).

[136] Nikhil Wagle and Ors. v. The State of Maharashtra and Ors. (07.01.2016 - BOMHC) : MANU/MH/0010/2016.

[137] Supra at 3; Page no 9.

answered in the negative in the case of Bonny D'Souza[138] by saying that there is no minimum amount that needs to be withdrawn for a test. The plain reading of section 185 sets the artificial limit of alcohol at 30 mg per 100 ml of blood. Interpreting this in a way to say that the minimum amount of blood to be withdrawn is 100 ml would be wrong.

A person cannot be booked under section 185 of the MV Act without a breath or a lab test.[139] In the case of Abhay Anand[140], the accused smelled of alcohol and under this assumption, he was arrested under section 185 of MV Act clubbed with Section 279 of IPC (rash driving). However, he was not subjected to a breath test under section 203 MV Act or a lab test under section 204 MV Act. The pre-requisite to arresting a person under section 185 MV Act is the proving of alcohol content in the blood to be over the allowed 30 mg per 100 ml. Since, the officers present at the scene forgot this sine quo non step, the accused was set free.

CONCLUSION

This paper remains in draft form, and hence any broad conclusions would be premature. The results show a moderate effect of the anti-drunken driving campaign on deaths and accidents, and changes in the incidence of drunken driving broadly consistent with a simple model of utility of potential drunken drivers. Some results—in particular the substantial spillovers from drunken driving enforcement both across and within police stations—are not well captured by the model and suggest that more complex dynamics are at work. The results presented in this draft are the main, but not the only outcomes of the drunken driving study. In particular, changes in accidents and drunken driving incidence over time during the course of the program await further analysis. The fact that decreases in accidents and deaths are strongest after the program suggests that these dynamics, driven by delayed adaptations in public and/or police behavior may be

[138] Supra at 13; Page no 19.
[139]MANU/KA/0551/1998.
M. Rajavalse v. State (23.07.1998 - KARHC) : MANU/KA/0551/1998 1999.
[140]Abhayanand Mishra v. The State of Bihar (23.09.1958 - PATNAHC): MANU/BH/0088/1959.

of substantial importance. Police graft and corruption is another element of the project for which further analysis might be particularly rewarding. A careful examination of surveyor reports, breathalyzer memory records, and court registers may yield some insight into what fraction of drunken drivers actually pay the official penalty and how many make a side payment to the police.

FALSE CONFESSIONS AND WITNESS LAWS: AN INTERNATIONAL COMPARISON WITH A FOCUS ON INDIA

Dr. JayKumar Bhongale[141]
Ms. Saheli Chakraborty[142]

ABSTRACT

False confessions and incorrect witness statements are major issues in the criminal justice system, leading to wrongful convictions and miscarriages of justice. Legal systems around the world have been grappling with these problems and implementing laws and regulations to prevent them from happening. In this article, we will take a closer look at false confessions and witness laws, with a particular focus on India. We will examine how the Indian legal system compares to international standards, what measures are being taken to address the problem of false confessions and incorrect witness statements, and what further steps can be taken to ensure that justice is served.

1. INTRODUCTION TO THE ISSUE OF FALSE CONFESSIONS IN CRIMINAL JUSTICE

False confessions have been a pervasive issue in criminal justice systems around the world. When a criminal suspect confesses to a crime, it can often be seen as a "smoking gun" by law enforcement and the courts, leading to a swift conviction. However, not all confessions are truthful. In some cases, suspects may confess to crimes they did not commit due to various pressures, such as coercion, intimidation, or manipulation by law enforcement officials. These false confessions can result in the conviction and imprisonment of innocent individuals while allowing the true perpetrators to escape

---

[141] Assistant Prpfessor at BVDU New Law College, Pune
[142] Author is a student of BVDU New Law College, Pune

justice.[143] The issue of false confessions is particularly relevant in India, where the legal system has been criticized for a lack of safeguards against coerced confessions and witness tampering. In this article, we will discuss the issue of false confessions in criminal justice, and examine the laws and practices in different countries, with a focus on India. By understanding the causes and consequences of false confessions, we can work towards creating a fairer and more effective criminal justice system that upholds the rights of all individuals.

2. THE PROBLEM WITH RELYING ON CONFESSIONS AS EVIDENCE

Confessions have often been viewed as the most reliable form of evidence in criminal cases. However, studies have indicated that false confessions are more common than one would expect. In fact, false confessions have played a major role in wrongful convictions in many countries, including India.[144]

One of the main problems with relying on confessions is that they can be coerced or even fabricated. Police officers may use physical or psychological pressure to extract a confession, particularly from vulnerable suspects who may not fully understand the implications of making a confession. In some cases, confessions may be the result of promises of leniency or threats of harsher punishment.

The issue with false confessions is particularly concerning in India, where police interrogation methods have been criticized for being coercive and even abusive. Reports have shown that suspects are often subjected to torture, and confessions are extracted through physical violence or the threat of violence. In addition, the lack of procedural safeguards means that confessions extracted under duress are often admissible in court.

---

[143] Sneha Mahawar, 'All You Need to Know about False Confession' (*iPleaders*, 12 April 2022) <https://blog.ipleaders.in/all-you-need-to-know-about-false-confession/> accessed 12 April 2023.

[144] 'Perception of False Confessions in India and Other Countries : An Insight - IPleaders' <https://blog.ipleaders.in/perception-false-confessions-india-countries-insight/> accessed 12 April 2023.

As a result, it is important to recognize the limitations of confessions as evidence and to ensure that proper procedures are in place to prevent the use of coerced or false confessions in court. This includes the implementation of safeguards such as the right to legal counsel and the recording of interrogations. By doing so, we can help ensure that justice is served and that innocent individuals are not unjustly convicted.

3. AN OVERVIEW OF WITNESS LAWS IN DIFFERENT COUNTRIES

Witness laws vary across different countries, and it is important to have a good understanding of these laws in order to ensure fair and just legal proceedings. In the United States, for example, the witnesses are required to take an oath before testifying in court, and the witness testimony can be challenged by the defense as well as the prosecution. The witness can be cross-examined to test their credibility and the weight of their testimony.[145]

In India, the Indian Evidence Act of 1872 governs the rules of evidence in legal proceedings. Witnesses in India are required to take an oath or affirm that they will tell the truth, and the witness testimony can be challenged by the cross-examination of the opposing counsel. However, there are some differences in the laws governing witnesses in India, such as the prohibition of leading questions and the use of leading questions only in certain circumstances.

In Canada, the laws regarding witnesses are governed by the Canada Evidence Act [146], which sets out the rules for the admissibility of evidence in court. The witness can be cross-examined, and the opposing counsel can also ask questions to test the credibility and reliability of the witness testimony.

It is important to note that witness laws can vary significantly from country to country and it is important to understand these differences, particularly when dealing with

---

[145] Brandon L Garrett, 'The Substance of False Confessions' (2009) 62 Stanford Law Review 1051 <https://heinonline.org/HOL/Page?handle=hein.journals/stflr62&id=1059&div=&collection=>.
[146] R.S.C., 1985, c. C-5_

international legal proceedings. In cases where false confessions are made, it is important to ensure that the witness testimony is reliable and credible, as false confessions can have severe consequences for the accused.

4. A CLOSER LOOK AT INDIA'S WITNESS LAWS AND THEIR EFFECTIVENESS IN PREVENTING FALSE CONFESSIONS

India's witness laws have undergone significant changes in recent years, with the introduction of the Code of Criminal Procedure (Amendment) Act 2008 and the Indian Evidence (Amendment) Act 2002. These laws aim to provide greater protection to witnesses and prevent undue influence or pressure from law enforcement officials.[147] However, despite these legal safeguards, false confessions continue to be a problem in India's criminal justice system. One reason for this is the lack of effective implementation of witness protection laws, which can leave witnesses vulnerable to intimidation or harassment.

Another issue is the prevalence of custodial torture and abuse, which can lead to innocent individuals being coerced into confessing to crimes they did not commit. In addition, the use of polygraph tests and other forms of unreliable evidence can also contribute to false confessions.

To address these problems, there is a need for greater awareness and education among law enforcement officials, judges, and other stakeholders about the risks and consequences of false confessions. There is also a need for better training and support for witnesses, and for more effective monitoring and enforcement of witness laws.

---

[147] 'False Confessions Analysis' (*International Journal of Law Management & Humanities*) <https://www.ijlmh.com/paper/false-confessions-analysis/> accessed 12 April 2023.

Overall, while India's witness laws provide some protections against false confessions, there is still much work to be done to ensure that these laws are effectively implemented and enforced, and that innocent individuals are not wrongfully accused or convicted.[148]

5. THE PSYCHOLOGICAL FACTORS THAT LEAD TO FALSE CONFESSIONS

False confessions can be a major problem in the criminal justice system, and it is important to understand the psychological factors that can lead to them. There are several reasons why someone might falsely confess to a crime they did not commit.

One factor is coercion or pressure from law enforcement, which can involve tactics such as threatening or intimidating the suspect, promising leniency in exchange for a confession, or even physical abuse. This can lead to a false confession out of fear or desperation.

Another factor is the vulnerability of the suspect, such as age, mental health, or low IQ. These factors can make a suspect more likely to confess to a crime they did not commit, either because they don't fully understand the consequences of confessing or because they are more susceptible to pressure from law enforcement.[149]

Finally, there are cases where the suspect may believe they actually committed the crime due to memory distortion or confusion caused by leading questions or suggestive interrogation techniques.

It is important for legal systems to recognize these psychological factors and take steps to prevent false confessions from occurring. This can include better training for law enforcement, establishing clear guidelines for interrogation techniques, and ensuring suspects have access to legal representation during questioning. By addressing these factors, we can improve the accuracy and fairness of the criminal justice system.

---

[148] 'False Confession - an Overview | ScienceDirect Topics' <https://www.sciencedirect.com/topics/psychology/false-confession> accessed 12 April 2023.

[149] Saul M Kassin, 'The Social Psychology of False Confessions' (2015) 9 Social Issues and Policy Review 25 <https://onlinelibrary.wiley.com/doi/abs/10.1111/sipr.12009> accessed 12 April 2023.

6. THE ROLE OF LAW ENFORCEMENT AND INTERROGATIONS IN ELICITING FALSE CONFESSIONS

The role of law enforcement and interrogations cannot be ignored when it comes to eliciting false confessions. The way in which an interrogation is conducted can have a significant impact on the outcome, and many factors can influence the way in which a suspect may respond.[150]

For example, in some cases, suspects may be threatened or physically abused, leading them to feel coerced into confessing to a crime they did not commit. Additionally, the use of leading questions or false promises can also influence a suspect to provide a false confession.[151]

It's important to note that law enforcement agencies often have a difficult job when it comes to investigating crimes and bringing criminals to justice. However, it's important that they adhere to ethical standards when conducting interrogations and do not engage in practices that may result in false confessions.

In many countries, including India, there is a growing awareness of the need for training law enforcement officials to conduct interrogations in a way that does not violate the rights of suspects or lead to false confessions. By implementing best practices in interrogation techniques, law enforcement agencies can help to ensure that justice is served and that innocent individuals are not wrongfully convicted.

7. THE IMPACT OF FALSE CONFESSIONS ON WRONGFUL CONVICTIONS

False confessions are a major cause of wrongful convictions around the world. It is unfortunate that innocent individuals may confess to a crime they did not commit due to coercion, pressure, or even psychological manipulation by law enforcement officials.

---

[150] Garrett (n 4).

[151] 'Perception of False Confessions in India and Other Countries : An Insight - IPleaders' (n 3).

Once a confession is obtained, many times it is used as evidence to build a case against the accused, leading to their conviction and sentencing.[152]

There are several reasons why false confessions occur. One common reason is that suspects may feel intimidated or threatened by law enforcement officials, leading them to confess to crimes they did not commit. Additionally, some individuals may have a mental health condition or cognitive disability that makes them more vulnerable to being coerced into confessing.

The consequences of false confessions go beyond wrongful convictions. Such confessions can also lead to a lack of trust in the criminal justice system, undermining its legitimacy and causing the public to question the fairness and integrity of the process.[153]

To prevent false confessions, it is essential to have robust witness laws that protect the rights of suspects and ensure that confessions are obtained voluntarily and without coercion. In India, for example, the law requires that confessions be made before a magistrate and not law enforcement officials, and that the confession be made voluntarily and without any coercion.

By understanding the impact of false confessions on wrongful convictions and ensuring that witness laws protect against such practices, we can work towards a more just and equitable criminal justice system.[154]

8. POSSIBLE SOLUTIONS TO PREVENT FALSE CONFESSIONS

False confessions are a significant problem in the criminal justice system, leading to wrongful convictions and loss of liberty for innocent individuals. Therefore, it is

---

[152] 'Studying Wrongful Convictions: Learning from Social Science Symposium: What Criminal Law and Procedure Can Learn from Criminology 7 Ohio State Journal of Criminal Law 2009-2010' <https://heinonline.org/HOL/LandingPage?handle=hein.journals/osjcl7&div=5&id=&page=> accessed 12 April 2023.

[153] Brandon L Garrett, 'Wrongful Convictions' (2020) 3 Annual Review of Criminology 245 <https://doi.org/10.1146/annurev-criminol-011518-024739> accessed 12 April 2023.

[154] 'Suspect Interviews and False Confessions - Gisli H. Gudjonsson, John Pearse, 2011' <https://journals.sagepub.com/doi/abs/10.1177/0963721410396824?journalCode=cdpa> accessed 12 April 2023.

important to explore possible solutions to prevent false confessions. One solution is to improve the training of police officers and interrogators, emphasizing the importance of obtaining accurate information rather than simply securing a confession. This can be achieved through the use of evidence-based interrogation techniques that rely on building rapport and trust with the suspect, rather than using coercive or deceptive methods. Additionally, recording the entire interrogation process can help prevent false confessions by providing an objective record of what was said and done during the interrogation. This can also help hold police officers accountable for any misconduct during the interrogation process.[155] Another solution is to provide suspects with legal representation during the interrogation.[156]This can help ensure that their rights are protected and can prevent police officers from using coercive or deceptive tactics to obtain a confession. Finally, reforming the criminal justice system to place a greater emphasis on evidence-based decision-making, rather than relying solely on confessions, can help prevent false confessions and improve the accuracy of criminal investigations.

9. THE IMPORTANCE OF FAIR AND JUST CRIMINAL JUSTICE SYSTEMS

A fair and just criminal justice system is fundamental to any democratic society. The rights of the accused, the victims, and the state must be balanced to ensure that justice is served. False confessions and witness testimonies can lead to the conviction of innocent individuals, which is a grave injustice that cannot be corrected once the damage is done. Therefore, it is essential that criminal justice systems around the world prioritize the accuracy and reliability of evidence and testimony.

In India, for instance, the laws surrounding witness testimony have recently been amended to make it easier for prosecutors to secure a conviction. However, this has also led to concerns that innocent individuals may be wrongly convicted due to false

[155] Kassin (n 8).

[156] Richard A Leo, 'False Confessions: Causes, Consequences and Implications' (1 January 2009) <https://papers.ssrn.com/abstract=1328623> accessed 12 April 2023.

testimony.[157] The importance of ensuring that the rights of the accused are protected cannot be overstated, and it is crucial that criminal justice systems are designed to prevent false confessions and witness testimonies from being used as evidence. In addition to these structural issues, there are also concerns about the training and education of those working within the criminal justice system. Law enforcement officials, prosecutors, judges, and defense attorneys all require specialized training to ensure that they can effectively carry out their roles and responsibilities. Without proper training and education, mistakes can be made, and innocent individuals may be wrongly convicted.[158]A fair and just criminal justice system is vital to ensuring that justice is served. The accuracy and reliability of evidence and testimony must be prioritized, and the rights of the accused must be protected. By working to address these issues, criminal justice systems around the world can help to prevent false confessions and witness testimonies from leading to the wrongful conviction of innocent individuals.

LANDMARK JUDGEMENTS

1. Anukul Chandra Pradhan v. State of Orissa (1999)[159]: The Supreme Court of India observed that it is not uncommon for an innocent person to make a confession due to police harassment or coercion. The court highlighted that the accused must be given the opportunity to recant or retract the confession, and failure to do so would amount to a violation of their rights.

2. State of Rajasthan v. Ramanand (2003)[160]: In this case, the Rajasthan High Court held that the burden of proof lies with the prosecution to establish that the accused made a voluntary confession. The court emphasized that a confession obtained under duress or coercion cannot be the sole basis for conviction.

---

[157] Kassin (n 8).
[158] 'Perception of False Confessions in India and Other Countries : An Insight - IPleaders' (n 3).
[159] AIR 1999 SC 3342
[160] (2003) 8 SCC 180

3. State of Maharashtra v. Praful B. Desai (2003)[161]: The Bombay High Court observed that the right to fair trial includes the right to not incriminate oneself. The court held that a confession made by an accused person during police custody without proper legal advice must not be admitted as evidence in court.

4. State of Madhya Pradesh v. Bhagwan Singh (2005)[162]: The Supreme Court stated that a confession made by an accused person must be voluntary, and not under police coercion. The court recognized that custodial torture and intimidation were serious human rights violations, leading to false confessions and wrongful convictions.

10. CONCLUSION AND CALL TO ACTION FOR REFORM IN WITNESS LAWS AND INTERROGATION PRACTICES.

The comparison of witness laws and interrogation practices across various countries has shown that false confessions are a serious issue that needs to be addressed. The high percentage of wrongful convictions resulting from false confessions is a clear indication that something needs to change.

India, in particular, has a long way to go in terms of witness laws and interrogation practices. The use of physical violence and torture during interrogations is a violation of human rights and a disgrace to the justice system. The lack of legal protections for witnesses also puts them at risk of coercion and intimidation.

Our call to action is for reform in witness laws and interrogation practices worldwide, with a specific focus on India. Legal protections for witnesses must be strengthened, and the use of physical violence and torture during interrogations must be abolished. The implementation of best practices from other countries such as the use of video recordings during interrogations and the requirement of legal representation for

[161] (2003) 4 SCC 601
[162] (2005) 9 SCC 730

suspects and witnesses could also make a significant difference. It is only through these reforms that we can ensure that justice is served, that innocent people are not wrongfully convicted, and that the guilty parties are held accountable for their actions. It is time for us to take action and push for these reforms to be implemented.

HUMAN WILDLIFE CONFLICT – NEED FOR AN ECOCENTRIC REGULATORY FRAMEWORK

DR. JAYKUMAR BHONGALE*

MR. OISHIK BHATTACHARYA**

Abstract

Human–wildlife conflict refers to the interaction between wild animals and people and the consequent negative impact on people or their resources, or wild animals or to their habitat. The reasons for human –wildlife conflict include the growing population of humans and the encroachment of forest and consequent hazards created to wildlife. The inevitable consequence is the loss of life and resources of humans, and destruction of both wild and domesticated animals. Though there are numerous enactments, rules, regulations, policies and projects intending to prevent these conflicts and protecting both the sides, they have seldom proved to be effective. What is required is an eco-centric approach by keeping away the anthropocentric mentality so as to bring all the species to centre stage and ensure co-existence side by side without unevenly interfering into life, habitat, resources and surroundings of each other. The future is locked by the behaviour and actions in the present, this has to acknowledge and has to consider while taking action. Human-Wildlife Conflict is a threat to the future of all species and the only way to stop it is by preventing and reducing it in the present.

Key words: Human – Wildlife, Eco centric, Sustainable development

INTRODUCTION

As the name suggests human wildlife conflict refers to the direct conflict between wildlife species and human beings. This conflict is not new, as both have coexisted for millions of years. However, it has become more frequent in recent years resulting in casualties on both sides. The conflict is kickstarted once the urge for demands and need for survival conflict with each other. Both of this can be connected with either of sides. To be precise the human wildlife conflict starts either when human demands and conquests rise and wildlife fights to survive or when the wildlife erroneously attacks the human beings and human fights to survive. Either way the result is always what ecology does not want.

There is immense challenge against addressing the Human Wildlife Conflict as the approach which has to be taken in each incident is unique. Efforts to address this problem without fully considering the underlying socio-political conflicts often leads to temporary relief. The factors of culture and practice also need to be considered. Therefore, an interdisciplinary approach based on ecocentrism, coordination and collaborative conservation is needed to achieve meaningful results.

Human Wild Conflict: Evolution and Causative Factors

The origin of human wildlife conflict in India can be traced back to ancient period. Yet initially the animals were treated close to God and in certain cases worshipped. The wildlife was considered as something which was to be preserved. But with progress of time, the worship and respect were converted into hatred and hunting.[163]. With gradual passage of time and increasing suppression of humans, slowly the animals started to respond for their survival.

The medieval period marked an attenuation of this conflict as in addition to expanding encroachment, circus and animal exhibitions started. This led to more wildlife captivation. The process of catching animals was very dangerous and after captivating they were treated mercilessly. This at times took very dangerous turns, as these were more of the conflicts with dominance vs survival. Hunting and poaching was normalised and Kings of various kingdoms highlighted it as a matter of pride. Alongside religious influence also opened up and wildlife was infiltrated to catch various animals for using them for religious sacrifices and other religious practices.

The modern period offers no much difference compared to the past. The only difference is that new avenues of human wildlife conflict has opened up. As

*Assistant Professor and Research coordinator of Bharati Vidyapeeth Deemed to be University, New Law College, Pune.

** Student of BBA LLB SEM VII, Bharati Vidyapeeth, Deemed to be University, New Law College Pune.

[163] Iain J Gordon, "What is the Future for Wild, Large Herbivores in Human-Modified Agricultural Landscapes?" What is the Future for Wild, Large Herbivores in Human-Modified Agricultural Landscapes? (bioone.org)

modernization opened various sectors and industries, innovations started to dominate the world. The innovations hugely the mankind but emerged as the biggest disadvantage for the wildlife. Another point of origin of the conflict is climate change over the years. The climate change has affected the natural habitat of both human and wildlife species. As a result, both humans and animals have started to infiltrate into each other's habitat in order to find shelter and support for surviving the sever destructions, this towards an extend has contributed to human wild life conflicts. The climate change not only affected the shelter/habitat but most importantly affected the food chain which is also an important triggering point towards the conflict. We cannot just victim card the wildlife as the loss amongst the humans is also increasing, particularly if we take the case of India, we could see that the loss of crops and damage of land and human casualties were on steady rise during the past two decades.

Major Causes of the Conflict:

Anthropocentric Approach- Anthropocentric means regarding the mankind/human beings as the centre and most important element of existence as against God or animals. This approach has been the prime reason of human wildlife conflict. The human dominance is not a new thing, but on other hand has existed for ages. Animals were considered inferior and an element for domination by humans. The wellbeing of animals was a matter of least importance. Wildlife species were often relegated as mere hunting stuffs

The anthropocentric approach is evident even in the legal framework and guidelines involving animals. From the very habitat of wildlife, i.e., forests, it is human interest that always prevailed as apparent from the provisions of Indian Forest Act 1865[164] and followed by Indian Forest Act of 1878[165] and Indian Forest Act of 1927[166]. The Act of 1865 and 1878 were more focussed on establishing British control over the forest and thus hinting for ultimate control of human in the habitat for wildlife. The Act of 1927 was more focussed on the protection of the forest but if we move on to details

[164] The Indian Forest Act 1865, Act of Imperial Legislative Council

[165] Act no. VII of 1878, The Indian Forest Act 1878, Act of Imperial Legislative Council

[166] Act no. 16 of 1927, The Indian Forest Act 1927, Act of Imperial Legislative Council

there were large gaps in the Act which was meant for facilitate different illegal activities in the forest. The powers provided by the act ultimately hinted to exploit the forest which was habitat to different species. Just to facilitate human greed. Later Initiatives such as Indian Forest Policy 1952[167], Forest Conservation Act 1980[168] and National Forest Policy 1988[169] were more focusing to eradicate the exploitation of forest but was not completing successful in removing the dominating factor and in the end gave a slight edge to human needs.

Even the law directly involving wildlife, i.e., the Wildlife Protection Act 1972[170] does not give a different picture. The act aims to increase the scope for protection and preservation of wildlife but as other frameworks this act also contains loopholes and gaps when it comes for implementation. It consists of various provisions which could interpreted for human betterment and facilitating exploitation. Section 11(2) it exempts killing or wounding the wildlife species/animals in good faith. This is contended as a defence by offenders. Ironically what is good faith is to be determined by unilaterally by 'man' lest that be 'reasonable man. While the lack of clarity in the provisions has only added to misinterpretation. Moreover, the punishment provided under the act cannot be considered proportionate to the offence committed.

Human "Development Policies"- Development is change of particular thing from original state to a different state and it is part of evolution which mankind undergoes, so far, this what development is all about when it comes to development to human kind. Development always demands from its seekers as it never can be implemented without incurring any cost. When the cost is wildlife, the humans take anthropocentric approach and readily sacrifices the wildlife.

The infrastructure development projects often involve habitat and surroundings of wildlife, which eventually triggers human wild life conflict. For instance, the Kerala Silver Line Project[171] is promising faster connectivity throughout the state and

[167] No.13-1/52 F, The Indian Forest Policy of 1952, Policy of Ministry of Food and Agriculture.
[168] Act no.69 of 1980, The Forest Conservation Act of 1980, Acts of Parliament of India
[169] No.3-1/86 FP, The National Forest Policy, Policy of Ministry of Environment and Forest.
[170] Act no. 53 of 1972, The Wildlife Protection Act 1972, Act of Parliament of India.
[171] Report of Kerala Rail Development Corporation Ltd., submitted on March 2020.

considerable decrease in pollution, but yet the project needs 1383 hectares of land which also include eco-sensitive areas, wetlands, farm land and most importantly forest, which could alone destroy the habitat of wild life species and could lead to a new set of human wildlife conflict[172].

Yet another issue was involving Kerala, Karnataka and Union Government which was relating to highway[173] connecting both the State through Bandipur National Park which is home to various wildlife species. The night travel was banned as the night traffic through the highway at times causing accidents involving wild animals. The development of same highway is sorted for better road connection but the fact regarding risk towards wildlife species and human wild life conflict is forgone.

The commercial and economic development has also contributed towards human wildlife conflict. For enlarging the economy and commercialise various activities the wild spread initiatives were kept up front. The proposal of relaxation of Environment Impact Assessment in the recent Draft of EIA 2020[174] can be termed as the best example. An important thing like Environment Impact Assessment with so much relevance in protecting the environment where both humans and animals co-exist was proposed to be relaxed to set up more industries and targeting enlarging the economy is being criticized for the approach it has taken in destruction of the ecology for sake of commercial and economic development. Yet the union government is not fully withdrawn from the base idea and is pressing more for this relaxation.

Tourism development has also significantly contributed towards human wildlife conflict. In olden days the travel was confined with only for trade and in certain case for survival but with passage of time the travel tourism grew into a leisure activity that generated immense revenue in the economy. This led to expansion of tourism portfolio

---

[172] K.A. Saji, "Environmentalist raise concerns abort Kerala Silver Line Project that passes through ecologically sensitive area", dated on 24th June 2021, https://india.mongabay.com/2021/06/keralas-silver-line-project-could-be-an-environmental-disaster-in-the-making/.

[173] Ararthi Menon, "Much ado about a highway", dated on 8th November 2019, https://india.mongabay.com/2019/11/bandipur-much-ado-about-a-highway/.

[174] Draft EIA 2020, The Ministry of Environment and Climate Change Government of India, Gazzate of India Part-II, Section 3(ii)

by including eco-tourism, forest tourism and the like. The forest clearing, altering and deforestation were done for making it human friendly but the fact abouts wildlife animals were just ignored/neglected. The forest tourism reshaped and depleted the resources for wild life species and frequent human visit to the territory also caused various problems and hindered free use of the habitat for the wildlife species. The recent announcement of Telangana Government regarding the "Tiger Tourism" focusing on generating revenue from jungle safari boosting travellers through the tiger park[175] indicates revenue generating mentality from the forest habitat, this could however disturb the habitat of the tiger and also other species inhabiting which is being ignored.

Every development mantra comes with a demand and often it is mostly connected with losing the biodiversity and ecological balance. When the eco sensitive area are affected flora and fauna or the wildlife species are immediately affected. But the ultimate casualty will be the ecological balance of the planet. For instance, the Western Ghats region were termed as the Ecologically Sensitive Area and the adjoining villages were classified into Ecologically Sensitive Zones in Ghats Ecology Panel Report 2011(Gadgil Report) under the Chairmanship of Madhav Gadgil.[176]. The report suggested that the areas classified under the area and zone should not be altered or messed up with. The warning contained in the report strongly suggested adverse environment and ecologically impact including threat of human wild life conflict. The major reason for classification of the ghats into different area and zone on the basis of ecological sensitiveness is that it is home to hundreds of globally threatened flora, fauna, birds, amphibians, reptiles and fish species. It is also in consideration of the fact that the region is covering long distance with connecting various states and providing it with ecological balance. At present but most of States involved in the area are neglecting the fact and thus facing the wrath of the negligence. The Western Ghats now is described as

---

175 Swathi Vadlamudi, "Tiger Tourism on Nallamala Hills", page:5 of THE HINDU News Paper dated 15th November 2021.

176 "Report of Western Ghats Ecology Expert Panel", dated 31st August 2011, submitted to Ministry of Environment and Forest, Government of India.

'Restless Mountains, shattered live'[177] as it is clear that Government policies and ruthless exploitation by private entities have disturbed the lives of wildlife species located there in.

Extreme weather and environmental Issues - The weather and environment conditions play a crucial role to determine the ecological balance in which both human and wild life could co habit. The adverse effects of environment destruction is slowly reflecting in the form of mass disasters like earthquakes, flood, drought and landslides. The Inter-Governmental Panel on Climate Change in its Sixth Assessment Report submitted in 2021[178], estimates that world will reach or exceed 1.5 degrees C of warming within 2 decades that could make faster heating of sea and glaciers hinting at about more and more calamities affecting all the inhabitants including humans and wildlife. This could also mean that as the disturbance is caused by calamities could lead to direct encounters and conflicts between humans and wildlife for survival.

Population Increase- The population increase is yet another reason triggering the human wildlife conflict. The population increase in both sides i.e., human and wildlife species are factors which influences the conflict. The population increase in humans comes with various requirement, the most important being resources to survive, but this often is unable to be met and results into penetration towards the resources meant for the wildlife species, this result in depletion of resources in which wildlife species can rely. The ultimate outcome is conflict for capturing and retaining the resources.

Due to surge in population the options of inhabitancy have declined, this also kickstarted the migration and resulting encroachments into inhabitants of wildlife species. The result was the depletion of inhabiting space of wildlife species. The encroachments into habitat of wildlife species put humans and wildlife species close to each other which has also resulted in frequent violent interaction between both. The close inhabitants caused frequent visit of both groups into each other habitats, which

---

[177] G Krishnakumar, "Restless mountains, shattered lives", page:13 of THE HINDU News Paper dated 24th October 2021.

[178] Kerstin Stendahl, Deputy Secretary IPCC, "Report on 6th Assessment cycle", 2021, Inter Governmental Panel on Climate Change.

resulted in violent encounters, also frequent encroachments resulted in alteration of habitat for wildlife but it did not make the wild animals conscious about their boundaries and the same could not be expected from the wild animals. Thus, wild animals continued their routine visit to places and locality even if it was captured by humans, this at times caused hurdles and facilitated frequent human and wildlife encounters.

Frequent incident of wild animals attacking human in close border habitats has also indicated for the need for regulating interaction between both sides and need to regulate their living conditions which is closely lying against each other. Now, in certain exceptional situation the wildlife/wild animals population increase also trigger the human wild life conflict. In most of the cases the situation is different but as mentioned this exceptional situation also has to be analysed properly. The population increase in wildlife animals, surges their needs of resources as resources limits and the needs has to be met. The quest to survive and to find out new resources forces them encroach into human habitat to satisfy their needs. This at times causes human wildlife conflicts.

Wild Animals venturing into human habitat has caused widespread destructions not only to life but also to livelihood which starts the conflict. We could clearly get the situation when we analyse incidence of wild animals attacking the habitat including fields, house and other assets of the Humans. The shocking revelation of reported figure of about 10 years, where reported 124 major and other minor incidence of livestock and human life attack by wildlife animals[179] also indicate towards the same.

We could safely mention that population increase irrespective of side has its own effect on human wildlife conflict and is more or less an important triggering point of same. The population fluctuation related issues can be least controlled as so it is uncontrollable and need another conscious approach for the same.

Human population increase and related contributory causes is more alarming as this is often causing major issues related to conflicts between human and wildlife but as

---

[179] Saurabh Prashar, " In 10 years, wild animals on prowl attacked livestock 124 times in human settlements around 2 Haryana Forests, dated 22th August 2020, https://indianexpress.com/article/india/in-10-years-wild-animals-on-prowl-attacked-livestock-124-times-in-human-settlements-around-2-haryana-forests-6565924/.

mentioned it is in a certain way out of hand and uncontrollable, something which can ensured is the division of resources and handling the issues with more intelligent approach.

Impacts of human wildlife conflict

Disturbance to Ecological Balance - Every element in ecology should be balanced otherwise it could end up in various outcomes which might even extend to adverse outcomes. The species existing in the ecology are also an important element which should be evenly balanced. The ecological balance even includes the relationship between living things with its non-living environment. There is also food circle existing in ecology and following this food chain a balance is maintained. If one element of food cycle become extinct or not available imbalance to food circle and to ecological system as a whole.

The human-wildlife conflict certainly causes ecological imbalance as disturbing the same with interfering in the circle. Both human and wildlife are part of the bigger part of ecological circle and are essentially the vital elements to keep the balance. The human wildlife conflict essentially affects one of the side which ultimately affects the ecological balance.

The ecological balance has chain reaction and if one species is affected the whole circle goes down. The impact of the same is negative. This could be understood with example from 1920's where in Yellow Stone National Park the grey wolf was eliminated considering it as a harm but subsequently elk which was predated by grey wolf grew in population as their primary predators were not affecting them, this caused severe setback as there was full malfunctioning of ecology in the national park, the impact was also visible in other species. Later on, in 1995 the ecologist re introduced the grey wolf to restore everything. This particular example of Yellow Stone National Park we could identify the human wild life conflict as ultimately the humans decided that grey wolf was harmful and eliminated it completely, which damaged the whole balance. Thus, it is clear how human wild life conflict could affect the circle and ecological balance and how sever it could end up.

Moreover, the ecology is a basic type/part of biodiversity, which is a much bigger picture. The biodiversity is described or explained at three important levels namely, genetics, ecosystem and species all these work together to run Earth. The genetic diversity consists of variation of genetics and species diversity consist of species variation with combination of various species and ecosystem diversity consist of variation of habitat and living condition of species[180].

The biodiversity is important because it gives clues on how variation take place for each species. This on brighter side is also crucial when it comes to managing every species. The human-wildlife conflicts cause disturbances to equilibrium of biodiversity and it damages the basic balance of existence. When the equilibrium is shattered the variation of species cannot be analysed and this ultimately leads to imbalances.

Further, ecological balance is dynamic objective which has to be achieved and if it is achieved it ensures survival and existence of all organism side by side with sufficient balance which is required. On the other hand, the diversity as for biodiversity is also maintained. In short, ecological balance maintains the entire biota for the establishment of healthy environment which is as much required for survival and on the other hand ecological imbalances brings widespread destruction. Thus, the relevance to maintain the ecological balance is very high and it as much required for proper functioning. The human beings have a very crucial role to play in the process, since amongst the species humans are endowed with rationality to understand the need for harmonious relationship between organism and environment.

Destruction of Habitat- The destruction of habitat is an obvious impact of human wildlife conflict. The habitat is the natural home or surroundings of a particular species. Be it human or wild life species the habitat is necessary and crucial for survival. Without the habitat to live no species can particularly continue its existence because it is the basic root which connect every species to be reality and lifestyles.

Wildlife species require four basic components for an ideal habitat, namely- food, water, cover and space. If these components are present then the habitat is

---

[180] Richard F. "Genetic and Extinction". Biological Conservation, 2005, 126 (2):1-140.

complete for the wildlife species. When human-wildlife conflict occurs, there is direct effect on the either of these four components altering the very nature of habitat. The impact can be assessed through the elements of Successional Stage, Structure, Size of Area, Arrangement, Surrounding Landscapes, and Time of the Year.

Starting with Successional Stage, it signifies the predictable change in the plant community. Every plant community species undergoes changes during different course or quarter of time or due to fixed reason, these changes are as said predictable and is necessary for the evolution of the particular community and also for the species relying on it. Different species might consume it so it is important that everything happens as predictable. Now, human-wild life conflict is unpredictable which affects the successional stage directly, this may be because of the previously cited ecological imbalances or due to widespread encroachment which influence the successional stage. Next element is Structure, this signifies the structure of habitat where the species exist. Now every habitat has its own structure which is important to be maintained as it is very important to manage the habitat and its process, but the human activities particularly human wildlife conflict alters this structure resulting into very severe impacts. Taking an example of forest with thick trees covering it, this is also important for the forest to retain the humidity level but if as part of the conflict any alteration is made to the thick trees which is an important structure then this alteration damages all other species relying on humidity. Taking next elements Size of Area and Arrangements in the habitat are almost similar, as the size of area and arrangements are important and as crucial as other element. Firstly, the size of area if depleted could alter the movement and growth of wildlife species and secondly, arrangements refer to arrangements of resources in the habitat and which species could exist without any resources. Thus, human-wild life conflicts particularly leading to depletion of the same would cost the damage of the habitat and leading to causing harm to species relying on it.

Surrounding Landscapes as an element is important as is as much important as the habitat because it forms the environment and physical ambiance which is very important for the species existence. More dynamic the surrounding landscapes more are dynamic the species can grow and co-exist but as far the development needs of the humans are growing result is depletion of surrounding landscapes, this element leads more chance of human-wildlife conflict.

Finally, regarding Time of the Year as an element, this refers to the time of the year when each happenings occurs periodically and annually which is much important for the maintains of ecological balance and preserving the habitat but when human-wildlife conflict it will also affect the cycle which is much important preserving the habitat.

Thus, these elements and alteration caused to it by human-wildlife conflict affects the habitat thereby causing the destruction to it. The destruction occurs either way of direct destruction or fragmentation or degradation. The wildlife habitat is not the only habitat which is affected by the human wildlife conflict. Human habitats are equally affected. The wildlife species infiltrates to human habitats depleting human resources and damaging the lively hood of the humans leaving a long-lasting impact. There are many instances where the wildlife attack is faced not only in the village areas but also in city limits causing destruction.

Fight for Survival- The fight for survival is yet another obvious impact of human-wildlife conflict. As and when any conflict occurs the nearest outcomes would be to somehow survive it, sometimes even at any cost the survival is given greater importance. The survival as a concept is wider and is often kick started by the weaker points in a conflict, this is because the weaker links would not be able to fight back and withstand the aggression from the opposite side, thus, the most obvious choice would be to gather all the resources and somehow survive the aggression from opposite side.

In a human-wildlife conflict the fight for survival may be from either end, depending on the situation. The fight for survival from the part of wildlife is either in the form of attack of humans regain the resources for their existence or migration from the habitat or place of aggression to a different habitat. The second instance is seldom resorted as wildlife species prefer to stay where they belong and fight back from there.

The aggressive fight for survival takes extreme turns leading to extinction of wildlife species. Lethal management is most often the methodology to fight back the wildlife species. Lethal management generally involve killing or sufficiently destructive mechanism used against the wildlife animals/species[181]. Culling is a narrower concept involved in the same, while the culling is done as a precaution against the spread of diseases or virus and its instance can be mostly seen in Zoo as in to protect the visitors or the remaining species from catching the virus.

The lethal management is State sponsored in most of the cases, but this is done with an intent to protect the humans and their livelihood. The instance of Gray Wolf in North America[182] can be considered here where in it faced government sponsored lethal management initiative, i.e., it was killed or brought to complete extinction on account of the threat it posed to citizen of the country. The same fate was met by Zanzibar Leopard and White Shark as they were attacked with the government sponsored lethal management initiatives.

In certain cases, the need is so high that without the any such initiatives the humans are not able to withstand. There are many instances where wild animals particularly elephants attack the fields and farm sector and as a prohibitory measure government resort to electric fencing to prohibit the movement. This could even lead to death of elephants but the necessity and fight for survival demands the same. The recent Kerala High Court Judgment[183] of allowing shooting permission and licence to farmers on account to shoot down the wild boars attaching their field also indicates the necessity and fight for survival.

The problem with the fight for survival is that it can leading aggravation and recurrence of conflict and may lead to the wipe out of species involved either way. The fight for survival continues to greater limits and it never stops on achieving a specific goal but it continues till extinction of either end of the conflict.

---

[181] S Vantassel, 'Wildlife management professionals need to redefine the terms: Lethal control, nonlethal control, and live trap' (2012) 6(2) Human-wildlife Interactions 335.
[182] Musiani and Paquet (n. 8) at 50.
[183] MT Thomas and Ors. v. State of Kerala and Ors., WP(C). No. 8442 of 2010.

How to balance and mitigate human wildlife conflicts?

Wildlife Conservation- This is the best cure when it comes to human-wildlife conflict. It is very important to preserve the wildlife species, and if is taken up seriously, inevitably the human-wildlife conflict would go down. Wildlife conservation indicates the protection of species be it plants or animals in their natural habitat which helps to complete the cycle and it ensures that the balance would not be spoiled.

The importance of conservation is underlined by the fact that human population is increasing every day while wildlife population is on the decline. Wildlife conservation approaches inject the balance of life cycle into the ecology. This could be illustrated with a simple example where in a food cycle which is part of life cycle an insect is eaten by frog and frog is eaten by snake and what will happen if frog is extinct the cycle is broke as in snakes cannot eat insects and thus a conflict would arise, slowly snake population would be low as there is no food and insects' population would grow as there is no predator. This situation could be only avoided with preserving the frogs which would complete the cycle and maintain the balance.

Currently, international organisation such as World-Wide Fund, Conservation International, The Wildlife Conservation Society and United Nations have taken positive step and active interest in conservation of wildlife species and to maintain public funds and other resources to achieve the same. International policies and initiatives are formulated with a view of preserving the species and preventing them from nor getting extinct. The goals of these bodies have always been the preservation of the ecology and its species and also to promote awareness and education on the issue so as to get better response.

Nevertheless, the global initiatives have not reached its full extend and is lacking in the implementation part. Most of the projects are for preserving the endangering species while all other species who are fast running into this category are neglected and as and when they enter the endangering category, the project for preserving them is kick started. A reversal of approach i. e. Preserving all species and not only the endangering species is required. A uniform implementation scheme is also required so as to ensure that global efforts are replicated at national levels.

Role of Individual, State and NGOs

Role of Individual- Every Individual has a big role to play in preventing human-wildlife conflict. The best action a person can take is to remain within the limit of ecological boundaries and not to interfere with the habitat of wildlife species. All the encroachments and destruction of the wildlife habitat have to be stopped and the unwanted quest for more resources than one's own need has to be limited.

Moreover, individual should not interfere in the activities which wrongly interfere with the wildlife species. Further, entertaining activities such as circus or zoo and sports activities such as leisure hunting should all be stopped as these wrongly use the wildlife species and treat them mere as entertaining activities or commodities.

Role of State- State is committed to every citizen and subject of its, thus, they should protect them. Apart from this State should also take active interest in prohibiting its subjects/citizen from infiltrating into wildlife. The State should focus on development but not on account of destruction of environment, surrounding and habitat which supports wildlife. The projects costing such destruction should be dropped. More inclusive approach has to be taken in case of wildlife as until now wildlife is not considered as something which needs protection or on the other hand, they are considered to be things which ought to be dominated. The approach should be treating wildlife species as similar to humans which should be give importance. If each state takes initiative to cover all the species under its territorial jurisdiction, then it can be great change.

Role of NGOs- The NGOs have an important role to play in preventing or reducing human-wildlife conflicts. The NGOs have actively protested against the government. They could also educate large population for the need of preventing the conflicts.

Adoption of Eco Centric Approach - The Eco Centric approach targets to keep the environment or nature at the centre for all decision making. It completely focusses on environment and not particularly to what humans requires. It also indicates that anthropocentric approach which keeps humans at its centre of focus has to be replaced with a philosophy of inclusive habitat and environment.[184] This approach highlights the need of preserving all the layers of Earth and it consequently presses for preserving and maintaining ecological balance which would ensure the cycle goes on and no disturbance is caused which break the cycle.

Further, Ecocentrism helps the humans to realise their duties towards nature and it gets centred to solve all the related crisis, ecocentrism remind us that all the humans and non-humans including all species are essentially interdependent and are related to each other[185]. Naturally, a common empathy is developed towards fellow cohabitants irrespective of the species difference which would thus limit the anthropocentrism present in the humans. Gradually, unwarranted actions from human side would decline as mutual respect developed. Every species would be able to remain in its boundaries and lead a resource full life.

Ecocentrism is not anti-humanism but inclusive of every species. It is in consonance with anthropocentrism yet different from it in terms of its objectives. Objectives of anthropocentrism are- maintaining essential ecological process for human survival, preserving genetic diversity for protection of human resources and ensure sustainable utilization of species for human community. On contrary the major objective of ecocentrism is inter-species justice alongside inter-human justice which highlights the bigger picture of including all the species into the ecology and it also interpret the reality that humans were not alone during all the ages and should not be alone as on for existence of whole ecology.

Ecocentrism is not only for present or not only for correcting the past mistakes but for a brighter side is has a great impact on future. It lays down a path way for the future generation and links various factors and fill the gap. It ensures that preservation mechanism and environment or nature centre approach is taken so that the balance

---

[184] Curry P (2011) Ecological Ethics: An introduction (2nd edition). Polity Press, Cambridge, UK.
[185] International Union for Conservation of Nature and Natural Resources (1980) World Conservation Strategy: Living resource conservation for sustainable development, https://is.gd/NzzGT4 (accessed March 2017).

even though is disturbed in present it would not be so in future and at least the future generation would be able to lead a greater resource life cohabiting alongside with all other species.

Implementing Sustainable Wildlife Management- The sustainable wildlife management is the sound management of wildlife species to manage or sustain their surroundings or habitat. This involves recognizing, maintaining and controllably applying the existing resources[186]. This may sound lot similar to wildlife conservation but the concept is different regarding the approach. In simple words this could be explained by pointing out that wildlife conservation is mostly related to conserving wildlife from endangering so as part of that plans and policy are formulated to achieving the same, while sustainable management is focused on managing all the resources sufficient for the species to survive and planning for properly using it without wasting it and thus maintains balance form getting interfered with. We could however say that sustainable management includes wildlife conservation as part of managing and planning for the process. Thus, wildlife conservation is narrow when compared to sustainable management and is included in the concept.

Sustainable management is best cure when it comes to human-wildlife conflict as the sustainable management is directly addressing on lot of factors which initially leads to human-wildlife conflict[187]. Sustainable management not only helps to manage resources for the wildlife but ensures proper resources is available to the humans which thus avoid needs for encroachment or any involvement in the wildlife. This towards a greater extend cut out probability of human-wildlife conflict.

The key concerns leading human-wildlife conflict i.e. Safety-security, food security and diseases transmission can be solved with sustainable management as the sustainable management ensures optimum utilization of resources which in turn ensures food security. Sustainable management takes direct and firm action on the root

[186] Kahler, J. S., Roloff, G.J., & Gore, M.L. 2012. Poaching risks in community-based natural resource management. Conservation Biology, 27(1), 177–186.
[187] St. John, F.A.V., Keane, A.M., Edwards-Jones, G., Jones, L., Yarnell, R.W., & Jones, J.P.G. 2012. Identifying indicators of illegal behaviour: Carnivore killing in human–managed landscapes. Proceedings of the Royal Society B: Biological Sciences, 279, 804–812.

causes of human-wildlife conflicts. It addresses the lack of resources in rising population among humans and check unwarranted encroachments in one others habitat. The human made causes such war, unrest, climate change is also kept in check so as to ensure that it might not cause any conflict[188].

Sustainable management mechanisms help in reducing or avoiding the human wildlife conflict by-

- Shared governance, education and awareness raising- The shared governance and education ensure all-round reach and helps in equitable use of resources.
- Recognition of local community with expertise and skills- The local communities can solve human wildlife conflicts by in situ biodiversity conservation and eco-friendly co-existence methods.
- Financial resources- The pooling of financial resources allows to utilize it for meeting the requirement and distributing at exact time.
- Relocation of communities- Relocation of communities from vulnerable areas in order to avoid possible friction from happening and to ensure that relocated communities receive better resources so as keep them surviving.
- Good land use and panning it correctly- Using the land properly to generate various other sources of resources and planning it correctly would ensure proper distribution and balance.
- Growing alternate crops and protecting it- Growing of alternate crops keeps up that balance in food and continue the circle and protecting it from possible attacks in order to keep up the momentum.
- Controllable lethal management and construction of barrier- Controlled lethal management and construction of barriers would ensure the balance in the ecology,

Thus, the sustainable management mechanisms are useful cure when it comes to human-wildlife conflict and adoption of it globally would ensure the reduction or prevention of such conflict and to keep both the sides protected in the ecology.

---

[188] Canavelli, S.B., Branch, L.C., Cavallero, P., González, C., & Zac cagnini, M.E. 2014. Multi-level analysis of bird abundance and damage to crop fields. Agriculture, Ecosystems, and Environment, 197, 128-136.

Conclusion

The fact goes without saying that wildlife conservation is an imperative which sustains life in this planet. But the sheer expanse in the population as well as lopsided perceptions on development remains as prominent threats to augmentation of forest cover and wild life conservation. It is a trite fact that forest cover is fast dwindling and wild life is pitted against multi - pronged threats. On the jurisprudential scenario, the evolution of animal rights and human rights and the ensuing conflicts and desirable convergence are now seriously deliberated around the world. A shift from anthropo-centrism to eco-centrism in developing sustainable mechanisms and models of forest governance would add the much-needed vigour in the quest for the symbiotic existence.

It becomes incumbent for the state to formulate ways to manage such conflicts through governance models on a sustainable basis. Now a days every single incident of causality to the life and property of human beings generates chaos. The intensity of the chaos has spiked to a level where the affected people dare to take law into their hands and has many a times took law into their hands and involved in destruction of wild life which they justify as acts for self-preservation. The governments find hard pressed between the hue and cry raised by the victims for compensation and the bounden duty fastened on it by various statutes to conserve wildlife. Hence it goes without saying that there is a social cost involved in such instances both visible as well as invisible.

The States have to design proactive programmes by involving the take holders including the non-state actors to redeem the main stream society from the prevailing information and knowledge asymmetry levels about the intricacies involved and design models of co-existence to harmonize the relations for enduring solutions. It is imperative that what the state has to strive is to explore the frontiers of inclusiveness having an appreciable effect on sustainable models of biodiversity conservation by integrating participatory approaches.

Introduction of Neuroscience in Juvenile Policy Making

DR. JAYKUMAR BHONGALE*

MR. OISHIK BHATTACHARYA*

ABSTRACT

A nation's youth are one of its most valuable resources. The law is a tool for helping youngsters reach their greatest potential. His growth is hampered by youth misbehaviour. So far, the law has responded by using both a carrot and a stick strategy. While many academic fields strive to comprehend young people and their actions, where neurology offers value. The lawmakers of our country are the products of the same society, a society which feels the criminalization of the juvenile system is the only way forward when dealing with the new breed of super predators. The act which deals with juvenile criminals in our country is the Juvenile Justice (Care and Protection of Children) Act, 2015 ("The Act"). The primary focus of the paper will be on the development of the juvenile brain during their adolescent years and how their psychological and neurological deficiencies mitigate their criminal culpability. The study uses an exploratory approach to examine how Indian constitutional law, legislative standards, and developmental neuroscience treat juvenile justice. The take on the methodical direction of juvenile responsibility and reform is presented in the paper's conclusion.

INTRODUCTION

A contradiction exists in the way our brain responds to small offenders. Sometimes, the image we conjure of them is that of helpless kids gone wayward. When we hold them in this light, where they are the victims of bad parenting, erroneous peer influences and hapless circumstances, we sympathize with them for their misfortune and immaturity. However, once the crime committed by them is no longer petty and all the sympathy

---

* Assistant Professor, Bharati Vidyapeeth Deemed to be University, New Law College Pune.

* Student of BBA LLB SEM VII, Bharati Vidyapeeth Deemed to be University, New Law College Pune.

that the society felt for them is consumed, we arrive at the opposite end of the spectrum. The same immature kids become the spawns of Satan with no scope for any improvement, who are *super-predatory*[189] in nature with the sole aim of corrupting the society with their obnoxious presence. The society then feels no compassion for these kids in this scenario and holds a hardened stance when it comes to dealing with them with respect to their crimes.

Reshaping juvenile justice is a never-ending challenge. Legislations are passed to address issues of justice and to prevent minors from being victimised while being identified as a delinquent. Law reform, is a continual process that responds to the ideals of society as they change. Fixing responsibilities, providing reformation to offenders or delinquents, and providing justice to the victims are the three main goals of the law.[190]

It is equally crucial for the law to identify the issues and comprehend the threats to societal values. Science and law can work together to a great extent to address the dangerous delinquent behaviour of kids and the subsequent negative influence on his growth and development as well as that of the nation. Research in the two fields should collaborate in order to comprehend a phenomena and develop solutions to the problems it poses.

CONSTITUTIONAL STANCE:

The conventional position is largely taken into account when determining who may be regarded a juvenile, and all of the county's resources are utilised to design numerous additional principles for the growth and protection of a juvenile. According to the 1989 UN Convention on the Rights of the Child, a "child" is defined as a person who is under the age of 18 unless the age of majority. The grundnorm stance in India may be found in the context of Article 24 of the Indian Constitution, which states that a child under the

---

[189] John Dilulio, *The Coming of the Super Predators*, Washington Examiner, November 27,1995, available at https://www.washingtonexaminer.com/weekly-standard/the-coming-of-the-super-predators (Last visited on October 4, 2019).

[190] Cohen, A. O., & Casey, B. J. (2014). Rewiring juvenile justice: the intersection of developmental neuroscience and legal policy.Trends in cognitive sciences,18(2), 63-65.

age of 14 cannot be employed in a dangerous job. Although the legal age of consent in this case is 14 years old.[191]

The court in "M C Mehta v. Union of India" determined that because construction work is a dangerous job, children under the age of 14 cannot be engaged. Abuse of children while they are still young is forbidden by Article 39(e). Article 39(f)" guarantees the children's healthy development and protection from exploitation According to Article 39 of the Constitution, it is the responsibility of the state to prevent abuse of children while they are still very young and to make sure they are not coerced into working in occupations that are inappropriate for their physical development and age.[192]

The act which deals with juvenile criminals in our country is the Juvenile Justice (Care and Protection of Children) Act, 2015 ("The Act"). It was passed against the backdrop of the horrific Nirbhaya Gang Rape[193] case, in which one of the accused was a minor falling short of reaching majority by a few months. The parliament felt that it was its duty to surf on the wave of emotions against antisocial teenagers prevalent in the country at the time, hence they brought in a law which not only violated the very preamble to The Act itself but also the basic tenets of the Constitution of India.[194] To add to that, The Act is also in contravention to all international treaties related to childcare and criminal rights that India is a party to.

The Act calls for the formation of a Juvenile Justice Board ("JJB")[195] for the preliminary assessment of the capacity of the children in the age group of 16-18 to commit crimes.[196]

---

[191] Ford, J. D., Grasso, D. J., Hawke, J., & Chapman, J. F. (2013). Poly-victimization among juvenile justice-involved youths. Child abuse & neglect, 37(10), 788-800. https://doi.org/10.1016/j.chiabu.2013.01.005.

[192] Goldstein, N. E., Serico, J. M., Romaine, C. L. R., Zelechoski, A. D., Kalbeitzer, R., Kemp, K., & Lane, C. (2013). Development of the juvenile justice anger management treatment for girls. Cognitive and behavioral practice, 20(2), 171-188.https://doi.org/10.1016/j.cbpra.2012.06.003.

[193] Gauri Pillai, Shrikrishna Upadhyay, *Juvenile Maturity and Heinous Crimes: A Re-Look at Juvenile Justice Policy in India,* NUJS Law Review, 2017.

[194] Constitution of India, 1950, Articles 14, 15, 21.

[195] Juvenile Justice (Care and Protection of Children) Act, 2015, Section 2(10), 4.

[196] Juvenile Justice (Care and Protection of Children) Act, 2015, Section 15.

The author will make an effort to convince the reader that adolescent criminal behaviour is a product of both their contacts with society and the steady maturation of their brains during their growth period.

Neuroscience of the adolescent's Developmental brain

The premise that the author wishes to set is that in order to come to correct decisions, the people who work in the juvenile process need to be aware of the changes that a child's brain goes through during his adolescence[197], an age during which a child suffers from risk seeking stimulations projected by the brain itself.[198]

The study of a child's brain development will help us say that *transferring*[199] a child into adult criminal system means punishing them for their brain's incapability of regulating their actions. In line with the set premise is the principle of penal proportionality[200], which states that people who are less capable of committing crimes should be given lesser punishments for the same.[201]

Scientists have come with certain development and conclusively said that a juvenile at the age16 has the ability to answer and think logically which is indistinguishable from a adult perspective[202] The first three years of a person's existence were thought to be crucial for brain development, according to specialists.

---

[197]Duncan, *So Young and so Untender: Remorseless Children and the Expectations of the Law,* Columbia Law Review, *102*(6) (2002).

[198] Juvenile Justice and Adolescent brain, available at http://clbb.mgh.harvard.edu/juvenilejustice/ , (last visited on October 4, 2019).

[199] *ibid.*

[200] Laurence Steinberg, February 6, 2015, *Sentences Should Acknowledge Juveniles' Maturity, and Immaturity,* The New York Times, available at https://www.nytimes.com/roomfordebate/2012/06/05/when-to-punish-a-young-offender-and-when-to-rehabilitate/sentences-should-acknowledge-juveniles-maturity-and-immaturity (last visited on October 4, 2019).

[201] The Hindu, September 6, 2013, *Justice and The Juvenile,* available at: https://www.thehindu.com/opinion/editorial/justice-and-the-juvenile/article5097614.ece (last visited on October 4, 2019).

[202] Macarthur foundation research network on adolescent development and Juvenile justice, less guilty by reason of adolescence 2 (2006),

Future intelligence and decision-making capacity would be determined by the degree of neural connections formed in the brain at the teenage time.[203] Over the last few decade neuroscientists have found two key psychology processes, myelination and pruning of neural connections, which continue during adolescence. Myelination is the disposition of a layer of fat tissue around nerve fibers because people are left with far too many neurons following the massive growth that occurs in the brain during the last years of juvenile life and once again just before puberty.[204] Certain neural connections in the developing brain are used more frequently than others as people learn, develop new talents, and move through life.[205] The less-used connections shrivel away over adolescence and into adulthood. Early anatomical investigations shows, different regions of the brain which are mature and completely myelinated and pruned at various periods, some relatively early in life and others over the course of several decades. Both times, it seemed that the brain areas in charge of essential bodily functions and sensory perception matured most quickly, but the areas in charge of behavioural restraint and control, risk assessment, decision-making, and emotion seemed to take longer.[206] The frontal lobe is where many of these higher level activities are concentrated. Using contemporary MRI methods, the outcomes of both of these processes may be seen.
The conclusion that an adolescent's brain is typically less myelinated and pruned than an adult's was shown conclusively shown in the late 1990s by UCLA researchers who proved that these processes persist well into early adulthood.

Http://www.adjj.org/downloads/6093issue_brief_3.pdf [hereinafter macarthur report].

[203] P.R. Huttenlocher, synaptic density in human frontal cortex: developmental Changes and effects of aging, 163 brain res. 195 (1979); p.r. Huttenlocher et al., synaptogenesis In human visual cortex: evidence for synapse elimination during normal development, 33 Neuroscience letters 252 (1982).

[204] Paul I. Yakovlev & andré-roch lecours, the myelogenetic cycles of regional Maturation of the brain, in regional development of the brain in early life 3-70 (Alexandre Minkowski ed., 1967).

[205] Ruben C. Gur, brain maturation and its relevance to understanding criminal Culpability of juveniles, 7 current psychiatry reports 292 (2005) (providing a brief review of This topic and its relevance to adolescents); see also staci a. Gruber & deborah yurgelun-todd, Neurobiology and the law: a role in juvenile justice? 3 oh. St. J. Crim. Law 321 (2006).

[206] *Id.*

In one study, UCLA researchers analysed the brain architecture of 10 healthy 12–16-year-olds and 10 healthy 23–30-year-olds using MRI scans. In a different study, researchers obtained MRI scans of healthy people at intervals of four years from 4 to 22 years old. The researchers observed a distinct pattern of linear increases in the volume of white matter detected in front area of the brain but noticed nonlinear changes in the volume of grey matter, despite the fact that there was considerable inter-individual heterogeneity in the participants' cerebral cortex growth. They observed regional variations in grey matter volume, with an overall tendency toward preadolescent increases and post-adolescent declines.

SCOPE OF NEUROSCIENCE IN JUVENILE POLICY MAKING

Recent advancements in brain research that examine concerns of responsibility and "blameworthiness" of young offenders have a growing influence on juvenile justice laws. Christopher Simmons, an adolescent who was convicted of murder in a case that used neuroscience to support the conviction, was supported by psychologist Laurence Steinberg of the American Psychological Association, who stated that "capabilities relevant to criminal responsibility are still developing when you're 16 or 17 years old."

An adolescent brain is fueled by unchecked and immature emotions. Any incident of a crime committed by a teenager who is intellectually superior to his peer is accompanied by the inability of the society to reconcile with the fact that an intelligent child is capable of committing an offence.[207] Society fails to understand that intelligence has nothing to do with the commission for a crime.

A scenario in which the brakes of a person's car fail and he ends up running over a pedestrian sleeping on the sidewalk will not attract criminal liability because it was beyond his control. An adolescent's brain has a similar working principle. They lack complete autonomy over their actions because of their brain's accelerator.

---

[207] Elizabeth Scott, Thomas Grisso, Marsha Levick, and Laurence Steinberg, *Models for Change: System Reforms in Juvenile Justice,*(2015) available at http://www.njjn.org/uploads/digital-library/MfC-The_Supreme_Court_and_the_Transformation_of_Juvenile_Sentencing-Sept-2015.pdf, (last visited on October 4, 2019).

The Juvenile Justice (Care and Protection of Children) Act of 2000 in India set the minimum age of comprehension at 18. Legally speaking, anyone beyond that age might be held entirely accountable for his or her behaviour. However, advances in neuroscience over the last ten years show that brain growth lasts until a person is well into his or her twenties.

What does science have to say about the Indian government's decision to allow 16 to 18-year-olds to be prosecuted as adults and given adult sentences? Simply said, science does not support the choice.

Multiple researches conducted in the field of juvenile neuroscience have revealed that adolescents are different from adults because of their brain being in its maturation phase.[208] The US Supreme Court through a series of landmark judgments has emphasised on the fact that children are *different from adults*[209] because of their inability to assess the consequences of their actions.[210] Most of the actions undertaken by children are the result of their *"transient immaturity"*. Thus, it can be conclusively said that adolescents who prima facie appear to have assessed the consequences of their actions can still not be given the same criminal culpability as that imposed on their adult counterparts.

A NEUROSCIENTIFIC VIEWPOINT ON THE PRINCIPLES OF JUVENILE JUSTICE

One method of determining a juvenile's culpability is through a normal standpoint. Whereas criminology aids in developing a better perspective for reforming sentencing guidelines. Legal branch cannot simply ignore the most current advancement in the field of neurology. Neurological standards can be usefully included into the formation of responsibility, rules and punishment policies, which should be more scientifically

---

[208] Salil Bali *v.* Union of India, (2013) 7 SCC 705, Subramanian Swamy *v* CBI, (2014) 8 SCC 682.

[209]Roper *v* Simmons 543 U.S.551 (2005), Graham *v* Florida 560 U.S. 48(2010) , Miller *v* Alabama, 132 S.Ct 2455, 2470 (2012)

[210] Hannah Pickard, *Choice, Deliberation, Violence: Mental Capacity and Criminal Responsibility in Personality Disorder,* International Journal of Law and Psychiatry, vol.40, (2015).

oriented. The main focus of neuroscience is on understanding the brain, how it develops, and a variety of related ideas. Understanding juvenile from a neuroscience viewpoint starts with knowledge of which parts of the brain are responsible for what functions, what are the various functions of the brain are, how they work, how old the brain is, and many other different ideas.[211]

Global advancements in brain research that explore problems of responsibility and blameworthiness of young offenders are increasingly influencing juvenile justice practises. Adolescents and young adults have traditionally offered difficulties for policymakers. Higher occurrences of criminal behaviour, drug use disorders, and the onset of psychopathologies are frequently observed during this vulnerable age. The most significant characteristics include a spike in dangerous behaviours, elevated levels of impulsivity and sensation seeking, increased sensitivity to rewards, and increased response to danger and punishment. When you're 16 or 17, your criminal responsibility-related capacities are still maturing. When should a teenager be regarded as an adult? Is a subject raised by legal concerns about the age of majority? While it is permissible for minors to be tried in adult courts, their brains are very different from those of typical adults.

Brain Age: The results of the Brain Age study can provide a valuable viewpoint when examining juvenile justice policies. Today's neuroscience employs a variety of methods to determine the age of the brain, not only by examining its physiological traits but also by examining its functional characteristics. Nowadays, data are collected via fMRI, and the data are then analysed using numerous so-called worldly ideas. It might be difficult to comprehend an adolescent's growth from a cognitive and emotional standpoint.

The dorsolateral region of the frontal lobe is an element of the cognitive control system. Although it develops more slowly than the social-emotional system, this system gives the social-emotional system control. The limbic midbrain system and the orbital frontal regions, which are both parts of the frontal lobe, are both included in the social-

---

[211] Cohen, A. O., & Casey, B. J. (2014). Rewiring juvenile justice: the intersection of developmental neuroscience and legal policy. Trends in cognitive sciences,18(2), 63-65.

emotional system. It grows much more quickly than the cognitive control system. The social-emotional system particularly regulates the brain's emotional state. Because of the rapid growth of this system, teens have an increased demand for rewards, greater need for sensation, higher emotional reactivity to both happy and negative emotions, and increased sensitivity to social cues. Through adolescence, the psychological control system develops and functions, which results in: "an increase in the teen's impulse control; better regulation of the emotional system; detection of options. Age is associated with a drop in impulsivity, sensation seeking, peer vulnerability, and problem-solving capacity".[212]

CLOSING REMARK

Science and law must work together to advance both fields. Especially while taking decisions regarding issues as sensitive juvenile's conviction neuroscience should be taking into consideration. Herein after the detailed oriented study, the researchers have reached the point of conclusion and have suggested some of the steps that should be taken into consideration to reduce the juvenile delinquency.

In India the concepts of Fragmented MRI process should start so that it can be used in juvenile cases which would further helps in mapping the brain development of the delinquent. Neuroscience is just not only the department of study of brain but the branch of psychology is also co-existing. Thus a juvenile welfare and rehabilitation fund should be established and placed at the disposal of the JJ Board of the specific location or area to be used by it for the ongoing rehabilitation needs of the juvenile or child in question. This fund should receive at least 25% of the fine money levied by the criminal courts in each location.

Aftercare programmes should be run by voluntary social organisations with the necessary government oversight and assistance in order to create a meaningful and beneficial aftercare programme to help rehabilitate the prisoners by assisting them in

[212] Cohen, A. O., & Casey, B. J. (2014). Rewiring juvenile justice: the intersection of developmental neuroscience and legal policy. Trends in cognitive sciences, 18(2), 63-65.

obtaining employment in various government and private endeavours. Probation and other community-based programmes should be favoured since they have the ability to guarantee better care and rehabilitation for young people in addition to being cost-effective.

We should work to change our culture so that no child commits a crime. We can all agree that circumstances are the main reason why many young people commit crimes. The researcher believes that, if this issue can be resolved, juvenile justice will, to a large degree, be resolved on its own. The law should be vigorously enforced. The complete Juvenile Justice Act, if honestly executed, can prevent situations like the Delhi gang rape by giving young people who might become criminals prompt assistance. The act itself is not the issue; rather, it is how it is being applied. The need of the hour is to ensure that the act's existing provisions are executed rather than amending it.

MARRIAGES IN THE SHADOW OF CLIMATE VULNERABILITY

DR. JAYKUMAR BHONGALE*

MR. OISHIK BHATTACHARYA*

The factors that lead to child marriage are being exacerbated by climate change and related environmental issues.

ABSTRACT

Demographic behaviour may alter as a result of how climate-change interacts with social, economic, and political influences. The relationship between environmental stress and marriage hasn't got much attention. We investigate the connection between the risk of marriage and extreme weather, such as heat waves and dry spells. We discover that girls and women are more likely to get married in the year of or the year after the heat waves. The relationship is highest for women between the ages of 18 and 23, and weakest for those between the ages of 11 and 14. We also investigate the idea that severe weather influences families to accept less suitable daughter marriage proposals. We discover that girls who get married in extremely hot weather typically end up with less educated men and poorer families. Similarly to this, men with less education who married during unusually dry years are supportive of partner violence more than other married men married in normal seasons of the year. These findings collectively imply that families who experience environmental shocks adapt by hastening the marriage of daughters or by settling for less ideal marriage offers. Such behaviours highlights the particular vulnerabilities encountered by women as climate change accelerates and are expected to have long-term effects on their health and well-being.

The relationship between dowry, arranged marriages, and climate change in different parts of the world is discussed in this essay. We contend that as a result of the economic difficulties brought on by climatic concerns, thus there is an increase in child and forced weddings. We come to the conclusion that, in order to adequately safeguard against

* Assistant Professor, Bharati Vidyapeeth Deemed to be University, New Law College Pune.

* Student of BBA LLB SEM VII, Bharati Vidyapeeth Deemed to be University, New Law College Pune.

climate change, attention should be focussed on how to resist the crisis thus protecting children from getting married due to climate vulnerability.

INTRODUCTION

Environmental changes have a significant impact on our health and wellbeing, including our sexual and reproductive health. The idea of sustainable development with a human-centered focus is seriously threatened by crises like climate change.[213] Climate change and global warming are occurring at an unprecedented rate. The repercussions of climate change, which might include poverty, relocation, and a lack of education, are particularly dangerous for women and girls. These are all connected to gender inequality and may make it worse.[214]

According to the Global Climate Risk Index, Mozambique, Zimbabwe, and Bangladesh are some of the nations most impacted by climate change and have some of the highest rates of child marriage. 53 percent, 34 percent, and 42 percent (respectively) of girls in these nations are married before they reach 18 and frequently have children in their early twenties. More than 39,000 girls marry as children every day, making up a total of more than 14 million child brides worldwide each year. The overall number of child brides in Africa, the continent most affected by climate change, could treble to 310 million by 2050, according to UNICEF. In some places, female genital mutilation (FGM), which involves the partial or complete removal of female external genitalia or other harm to female genital organs for non-medical reasons, is linked to child marriage. In addition to denying girls their basic rights, child marriage is also linked to increased prevalence of sexually transmitted disease.[215] Existing availability of resources and

---

[213] UNFPA, 'Getting to Zero, Towards Rights and Choices for All by 2030' (2020) <https://esaro.unfpa.org/sites/default/files/pub-pdf/unfpa_annual_report_web.pdf> accessed 12 February 2023.

[214] 'Child Marriage Links to Climate Change | Psychology Today' <https://www.psychologytoday.com/intl/blog/modern-day-slavery/202212/child-marriage-links-climate-change> accessed 18 February 2023.

[215] 'Child_marriage_and_environmental_crises_an_evidence_brief_final.Pdf' <https://esaro.unfpa.org/sites/default/files/pub-pdf/child_marriage_and_environmental_crises_an_evidence_brief_final.pdf> accessed 1 February 2023.

education are made worse by environmental issues such as climate change. The intergovernmental panel makes a caution regarding the increase in temperature which will be nearly about 1.5 degree Celsius and it will push many people in a helpless position.. Acknowledging and understanding the fact that environmental change is a having a great effect on the crisis of child marriage in an unstable and changing environment, so that human rights can be protected and steps may be taken, to increase resilience to shocks and the effects of climate change.[216]

Key Notes:

i) Every year, one in five girls are married before turning 18 in the world. Years of work had caused the practise to wane, but it now faces the possibility of increasing due to climate change.[217]

ii) The causes of child marriage, such as poverty, relocation, violence, and loss of schooling, are multiplied by climate change and other environmental problems, according to research and data.[218]

iii) Female genital mutilation, domestic abuse, and other types of violence are all greatly increased by child marriage, endangering children's physical and emotional health as well as their freedom.[219]

iv) In agricultural communities, which are also more prone to face the consequences of climate change, child marriage is a typical occurrence.[220]

The Link between Climate Change and Child Marriage.

Many children worldwide are now more in danger of child marriage as a result of climate change and other environmental challenges. The connections between the two have been established by research and data from international organisations like the UNFPA.

---

[216] ibid.

[217] 'How Climate Change Is Driving Child Marriages | End Violence' (*End Violence Against Children*) <https://www.end-violence.org/articles/how-climate-change-driving-child-marriages> accessed 1 February 2023.

[218] ibid.

[219] *Id.*

[220] 'Child Marriage Links to Climate Change | Psychology Today' <https://www.psychologytoday.com/us/blog/modern-day-slavery/202212/child-marriage-links-climate-change> accessed 1 February 2023.

Many of the regions with the highest rates of child marriage are also those with the worst environmental challenges brought on by climate change. Those with less wealth and access to resources frequently engage in the activity which is particularly in rural locations where residents depend on their surroundings for a living.

For some of the families that are impacted, child weddings are a method to reduce pressure or even a chance to acquire money or resources through societal customs like "bride price" payments to the families of girls or "dowry" payments to the families of males. This is especially true for rural inhabitants, whose livelihoods depend most heavily on the environment. According to studies[221], conditions like droughts and flooding are associated with an increase in child marriages.

Families and communities are uprooted as a result of environmental catastrophes and climate change. By 2050, anywhere between 50 and 250 million people might be at very high risk of being displaced due to the effects of climate change, putting more families and children at danger.

Following the environmental catastrophes, conflict often intensifies. Due to these, there are more incidences and threats of violence towards children, which may lead to child marriages in some households. According to research, the likelihood of females being married as children decreases the longer they attend school.

How climate change affects child marriages may be explained by three broad phenomena.

i) The first is the gradual loss of livelihood brought on by climate change's indirect effects. As a result of the vulnerable population's dependency on the environment they have to face lot due to climate change - agricultural producers, fishermen, and herders are among the most vulnerable communities on earth. There are fewer fish to be caught due to rising water temperatures. Farming and animal husbandry are almost difficult during droughts and floods. When families struggle financially, child marriage may be the quickest and most practical option to feed one fewer mouth while making money

[221] Margaret E Greene, 'Ending Child Marriage in a Generation'. https://www.fordfoundation.org/media/1890/endingchildmarriage.pdf (last visited 12 February 2023)

through dowry and bride costs. This relieves pressures on the family and scarce funds. Girls occasionally accept these suggestions without question since they perceive them as ways to make their life better as well.

ii) The second is unforeseen, severe weather events, which can dramatically alter a girl's destiny leading to total property loss. In 2019, when the cyclones hit there was huge migration of people who have been forced to flee their homes because natural disasters have destroyed their livelihoods and property. Reports[222] of child marriage surged by more than a factor of two as families were relocated to settlement camps. Many families that regarded child marriage as a means out of their difficult conditions had increased living expenses and lower spare income as a result of this abrupt instability.

iii) Protection; protection for the females, but most crucially, protection for the "honour" of the family, is the third related, and perhaps the most controversial, cause. For a variety of factors, including the confusion, interruptions, and lack of shelter that follows a natural catastrophe, the risk of sexual assault is increased. Girls and young women are also more likely to experience sexual harassment and assault in the camps because of privacy and security issues.

Therefore, many parents rationalise their choice to marry off their daughters before they are adults by citing protection from sexual exploitation. In fact, the UN notes that child marriage is a serious violation of human rights since it deprives girls of the ability to make decisions about their lives and bodies which, interferes with their education, and exposes them to higher risks of abuse, violence, and discrimination. In addition, some families have been driven to marry off their children if they are further seen in the exodus. These resources become scarce as a result of environmental catastrophes including wildfires, storms, floods, and droughts. Females are more vulnerable to sexual abuse when they must go further from their houses to get everyday essentials like water and firewood.

The cause why children are being vulnerable to climate change

---

[222] Dana Kirkegaard, 'Marriage in the Forecast: The Link between Climate Change and Child Marriage' (*USA for UNFPA*, 12 July 2021) <https://www.usaforunfpa.org/marriage-in-the-forecast-the-link-between-climate-change-and-child-marriage/> accessed 1 February 2023.

Here the researchers studies two continent Africa and Asia and understand the root cause of all the vulnerabilities. The researchers further tries to explain the problem in a simpler way. The lack of educational and economic choices leads to child wedding. Patriarchal ideologies consisting misogyny, as well as exacerbating social factors like poverty, economic instability, conflict, and humanitarian crisis are all pointed to as the root causes and aggravating factors that contribute to child marriage.

The Various consequences of Child Marriage.

Children who get married before they're adults are more likely to experience several types of violence. Girls suffer more than boys from gender stereotypes and discrimination due to climate vulnerability. Families often choose girls over boys when deciding which "mouth to sacrifice" in order to conserve family resources. Boys are easier to hire and can support the family, so families are more inclined to invest in them. Gender-based violence (GBV): Child marriage is a gender based crime and further constitutes actions, such as rape, domestic violence, and female genital mutilation. According to studies,[223] married girls endure more physical, emotional, sexual, and financial abuse than their unmarried counterparts. Girls who are married as youngsters find it difficult to leave an unhappy marriage because of their economic dependence on their spouses.[224] Intimate partner abuse is 50% more likely to occur for girls who marry before the age of 15 due to climate shocks, than for those who marry later. Additionally, they are more likely to experience domestic abuse and other types of violence, including sexual assault, at home. Child marriage may occasionally result from the stigma associated with having sex or from an early pregnancy brought on by sexual exploitation. 90% of adolescent births take occur in the setting of marriage, and problems related to pregnancy and delivery are among the top killers of females between the ages of 15 and 19.

---

[223] 'ADOLESCENT PREGNANCY_UNFPA.Pdf' <https://www.unfpa.org/sites/default/files/pub-pdf/ADOLESCENT%20PREGNANCY_UNFPA.pdf> accessed 13 February 2023.

[224] Sarah Neal and others, 'Childbearing in Adolescents Aged 12-15 Years in Low Resource Countries: A Neglected Issue. New Estimates from Demographic and Household Surveys in 42 Countries' (2012) 91 Acta Obstetricia Et Gynecologica Scandinavica 1114.

High infant mortality and mortality from childbirth: Early pregnancy puts girls' lives at danger; internationally, problems from pregnancy and childbirth are the main cause of mortality for girls between the ages of 15 and 19. Additionally, child brides are more susceptible to a variety of mental health issues, such as depression, which is frequently brought on by social isolation. Girls who are married off as young children are far more likely to have female genital mutilation (FGM) in many nations, particularly in Africa, which has the highest rate of FGM incidents. Children's physical and mental health are negatively impacted by the trauma of child marriage and the violence that surrounds it. As a result, they have higher rates of depression, femicide, suicide, and diseases like HIV. Although 2 million of the 7.3 million births to underage (18 years) females occur to girls under the age of 15, and young girls are more at risk for child marriage and teenage pregnancy. . Proof about the continuing and generational impacts of child marriage is required. The financial consequences of early marriage are included here.

Governmental Involvement: Government of India, Malawi and Kenya has tried to lower the number of child marriages by raising the legal marriage age in response to criticism from NGOs and civil society activists. These rules haven't had much of an impact, though, because they aren't being enforced.

It may be necessary for civil society to provide solutions through initiatives that combine social involvement and financial assistance. If girls and women make less money than males, it could be more economical to marry them off or abandon them. But if females obtain the right education, they may have an equal chance with men of finding well-paying employment. In certain circumstances, cash transfers and education subsidies have been tried to persuade families to keep funding their daughters' education.

The Remedies: SPEEDED UP ACTION IN COMMUNITIES AND POLICIES: Without tackling the climate catastrophe, child marriages and other types of child abuse cannot be stopped. In addition, child marriages and other types of violence must be included in policies and decision-making while tackling the climate crisis. A crucial first step in taking action is the growing corpus of knowledge that is being made available to decision-makers.[225] Strong action and advocacy from and within communities is essential in bringing about change, in addition to legislative and structural changes. People like Ayesha Hammam are fighting to alter community perceptions and bring about legislative change to prevent child marriage and encouraging people working around the world to eliminate violence against children. To expedite the understanding and action required to safeguard the rights and safety of children worldwide, the end violence community must continue to engage together across nations and situations with children and advocates.

Child Marriage Linked to climate shock and India: A retrospective viewpoint

The frequency and severity of climatic changes raise the protection risks for children and young people in India, including child labour, sexual assault, and child marriage. These are findings of the researchers which highlighted hazards presented by the consequences of climate change on kids and teenagers in the Indian Sundarbans region. One of the world's most climate-vulnerable regions is the Sundarbans area, which is situated in the Bay of Bengal. Economically disadvantaged families are being pushed into the most extreme types of poverty by environmental changes including rising sea levels and an increase in the frequency of catastrophic weather occurrences. Children and teenagers are thus more exposed to abuse and exploitation, such as child trafficking and child marriage. The researchers showed how parents or other adults in the Sundarbans expose their children to more violence because they are under stress due to the effects of climate change. Concerns about their house, finances, and ability to support themselves are just a few examples of these reasons. Many parents relocate in search of employment while leaving their kids behind. Children frequently miss school in these situations in order to work or assist around the house. The high incidence of child marriages and female trafficking in the Sundarbans is well-known. The marriage of young females has increased during the past ten years. Due to a lack of resources in the home to satisfy their children's fundamental requirements, parents frequently embrace these marriages.

[225] 'About' (*Brides Of The Sun*) <https://bridesofthesun.com/about/> accessed 13 February 2023.

Both boys and girls are at serious danger when they marry young since guys are required to provide for their families and are driven into the workforce at a young age. Girls face challenges such as adolescent pregnancies and educational limitations that threaten their future and put them in a risky position.[226]

PUBLIC DUTY UNDER INTERNATIONAL LAW

International Human Rights Law: All governments are required under international human rights legislation to defend the rights of women and girls. A number of international human rights documents express opposition to child marriage, either directly or obliquely. Some treaty monitoring panels are starting to incorporate climate change implications within their responsibilities.[227]

i) The Convention on the Elimination of All Forms of Discrimination against Women ("CEDAW"): Article 16(1) provides equal rights to men and women to enter into marriage and provides an equal right to "choose a spouse and to enter into marriage only with their free and full consent." Article 16(2) states that "he betrothal and the marriage of a child shall have no legal effect, and all necessary action, including legislation, shall be taken to specify a minimum age for marriage and to make the registration of marriages in an official registry compulsory.[228]

General Comment No. 21 on "Equality in marriage and family relations," published by the Committee on the Elimination of Discrimination against Women in 1994, recognised that men and women have the same legal right to get married as long as both parties have totally and voluntarily agreed. [229]The Committee on the Rights of the Child and

---

[226] 'Climate Change Increases the Risk of Child Marriages | Terre Des Hommes' <https://www.tdh.ch/en/press-releases/climate-change-increases-risk-child-marriages> accessed 1 February 2023.

[227] 'International Covenant on Civil and Political Rights' (*OHCHR*) <https://www.ohchr.org/en/instruments-mechanisms/instruments/international-covenant-civil-and-political-rights> accessed 13 February 2023.

[228] 'Cedaw.Pdf' <https://www.ohchr.org/sites/default/files/Documents/ProfessionalInterest/cedaw.pdf> accessed 13 February 2023.

[229] United Nations High Commissioner for Refugees, 'Refworld | CEDAW General Recommendation No. 21: Equality in Marriage and Family Relations' (*Refworld*) <https://www.refworld.org/docid/48abd52c0.html> accessed 13 February 2023.

this Committee jointly issued a broad proposal on harmful practises, such as child marriage, in 2014.[230] In 2018 the announcement of a general proposal from the Committee on the Elimination of Discrimination against Women was passed which addressed "[g]ender-related components of disaster risk reduction in the context of climate change." This is "the first text approved by a human rights treaty body that clearly and authoritatively determines how States must reconcile international human rights commitments into climate action," according to the Center for International Environmental Law (CIEL). **The Convention on the Rights of the Child ("CRC"):** The Article 1 of the CRC exclaims human being below the age of eighteen years unless under the law applicable to the child, majority is attained earlier."[231] The Committee on the Rights of the Child called for states to[232] "examine and, where required, change their legislation and practise to increase the minimum age for marriage with and without parental agreement to eighteen years, for both girls and boys" in a General Comment from 2004.[233] Furthermore, Article 24(3) requires all the state governments to take effective measures relating to the health of children.

International Climate Change Law: The likelihood of child marriage is clearly linked to the vulnerabilities brought on by crises, particularly crises that may be made worse by climate change, in a new but expanding body of international guidelines. There have been three resolutions against child, early, and forced marriages adopted by the UN General Assembly since 2013. The first resolution, passed in 2013, which asked for a panel debate and report on child, early, and forced marriages throughout the world, signalling a change to look at child marriage from the perspective of human rights.

---

[230] Comm. on the Elimination of Discrimination Against Women & Comm. on the Rights of the Child, Joint General Recommendation No. 31 of the Committee on the Elimination of Discrimination against Women/General Comment No. 18 of the Committee on the Rights of the Child on Harmful Practices, U.N.
Doc CEDAW/C/GC/3 1-CRC/C/GC/18 (2014).

[231] 'The Convention on the Rights of the Child: The Children's Version | UNICEF' <https://www.unicef.org/child-rights-convention/convention-text-childrens-version> accessed 13 February 2023.

[232] 'Crc.c.nor.Co.4.Pdf' <https://www2.ohchr.org/english/bodies/crc/docs/crc.c.nor.co.4.pdf> accessed 13 February 2023.

[233] 'Convention on the Rights of the Child' (*OHCHR*) <https://www.ohchr.org/en/instruments-mechanisms/instruments/convention-rights-child> accessed 13 February 2023.

The Sendai Framework for Disaster Risk Reduction 2015-2030, adopted at the Third UN World Conference on Disaster Risk Reduction in 2015, presents an example of a missed opportunity to address child marriage. Understanding disaster risk is the first of four priority areas in this framework, which "aims to accomplish the considerable reduction of catastrophe risk and losses in lives, livelihoods, and health". The framework acknowledges that women and children are disproportionately affected by disasters and calls for the inclusion of a gender perspective in all policies, but the only reference to gender that is made specifically refers to increasing women's ability to find alternative sources of income in post-disaster situations.

CONCLUSION

The research that supports the possibility that child marriage may rise due to climate change effects has been brought forth in this article. Although the study is primarily qualitative or circumstantial, it is consistent and expanding. Although more research is needed to determine the exact relationship between climate change and child marriage, governments are still required by existing international obligations to: (1) make sure that their response to climate change includes special attention and monitoring of the impact on women and girls, including any risk that climate change impacts will exacerbate or undermine efforts to end child marriage; and (2) make sure that efforts to end child marriage through some effective system which should be designed to respond to the ways where women and girls are affected by climate change. Assessment and monitoring the effects of climate change should be a part of efforts to end child marriage. The decision-makers should take into account, which portions of the nation are most affected by climate change, while giving different regions of the country priority for anti-child marriage initiative. These programs has to be modified to help those affected by climate change and those who have been displaced by natural disasters. There should be a track records of the occurrence of child marriage among those living in climate change-affected areas.

These are only a few of the numerous ways that climate change issues might start to be included in campaigns against child marriage.

RIGHT TO PRIVACY AND NARCO- ANALYSIS TEST

Dr. Jaykumar Bhongale *

Abstract:

The privacy is very personal because it is the power of an individual. The Constitutional of India guaranteed under Article 19 of the Constitution, freedom of speech and expression. Another article which is article 21 of the Constitution talks about right to life and personal liberty encompass the right to privacy of the individuals. The established process is that the limitation shall put on the ground which is specified under article 19(2) and not otherwise and second is that to curtail the fundamental right, legislation shall be passed by parliament of India. In the name of governance and public order state is violating the very right of privacy without providing any justification. So it means if state want to put the limitation on right to privacy state has to pass the law. Data and information of the individuals becoming public property and state is doing nothing.

Present article speak about the constitutional safeguard and state liability towards right to privacy, it will demonstrate the real condition of governing policy and insufficiency and inadequacy to promote the individual fundamental rights. The present article also speaks about narco-analysis test, its effect and legality in confrontation with Right to privacy.

Key Words: Narco-analysis, encroachment, mental torture, testimony, reliability.

INTRODUCTION

Law and technology are connected to each other fashionable manner because when technology fashioned law tend to have fashionable. The development of scientific technology annoyed the territorial and cultural boundaries existed in primitive society. Due to advancement in the field of technology law also has to surpass resilience power according to the need of the society. One thing is very important in the perspectives of legal jurisprudence that while using the technology shall not overlook the essential procedure connected with law. The technology shall not violate the basic rights of the individual which may couple with Constitution or may not be coupled with Constitution. Narco-analysis test may be useful for the investigating agency and government machinery but other hand it should not violate the basic right of the individual.

WHAT IS NARCO- ANALYSIS

The term Narco-analysis means ("anesthesia" or "torpor"). From the time immemorial man has tried to find out the cause of internal secrets. Narco technique is not new to the world; early period to the modernization man was used to the diagnostic and psychotherapeutic technique.

The drug sodium pentothal is better known as truth Cyril, is injected into a person. This allows a person to speak freely without any inhibition. Before the test, a psychiatrist and general physician will check whether the person taking the Narco test is mentally and physical fit. The drug is then given inside of foreign-sick lab or in the operation Theatre of a recognized hospital. An anesthesiologist will supervise the injection and then a forensic psychologist conduct the test by asking questions. The test is only meant to aid investigative efforts and is not always hundred percent effective. It is the combination of Sodium Penthatol and Sodium Amytal cautiously dosage[234]administered to the receiver and synchronized on the basis of health condition of the receiver. It is totally administered under the supervision of health experts including psychologist and physiologist. Narco test is the process applied by the investigation agency, certain amount of drug may be given to the suspected person or witness interrogation through prepared questions in the trance stage.[235]

The right to privacy, right to privacy is the integral part of right of liberty.[236] If there will be conflict of interest between rights to privacy and state interest then definitely preference will be given to the state interest, right to privacy is not unlimited according to the Supreme Court of India.[237] Because there is no cognizant control over the

---

*Assistant Professor and research coordinator at BVDU New Law College, Pune

[234] *Justice K.S. Puttaswamy and Ors. v. Respondent: Union of India (UOI) and Ors., MANU*, 2017.

[235] "IJFMT July-Dec 2011.pdf,."

[236] *Gobind v. State of Madhya Prade, SCC*, 1975.

[237] *Ibid.*

individual by him, it won't be treated as evidence irrespective that there was informed consent available and given by the subject. Any material or any output revealed through the Narco test then court will accept the evidence as defined by section 27 of the Evidence Act.[238] The reason to not accepting the evidence relating to confession made under police custody is that police agency may contaminate the procedure and may force to the subject. So Court will not admit this kind of evidence unless it is not cross verified.[239]

The criminal justice system is dependent upon the support of the people especially person call for investigation has to provide equal cooperation for investigation of the case.[240] It is not unconditional right it is the social responsibility to provide proper information to the investigating officer.[241]

FREEDOMS AND REASONABLE RESTRICTIONS

1. A law cannot said to be a reasonable law unless it will satisfy the balance between Article 19(1), (2) and Article 19(6).
2. The fundamental right having primacy status than restrictions[242], it means Article 19(1) shall be predominated as comparison to Article 19(2)& (6) but we should not ignore that rights are not absolute and allowed to make reasonable restriction. It means fundamental rights are fundamental and limitation shall not obliterate very essence of the balance assigned to Article 19 as a whole.
3. For the protection of the general welfare the individual right may be suspended with the help of reasonable restriction.

---

[238] Ajay Kr. Barnwal and Dr.S.N Ambedkar, "Narco-analysis Test: An analysis of various Judgements of Indian Judiciary," 19 *IOSR Journal of Humanities and Social Science* 52–7 (2014).
[239] *Ibid.*
[240] *Dharmapal v. State, MANU*, 2003.
[241] *Ibid.*
[242] State is allowing to make restriction on the freedom available under Article 19 (1), on the following grounds; these restriction given under Art.19 (2) to (6); including Article 19 (g) condition applied

4. Right under article 19 (1) is the asset of the individual and limitation from (2) to (6) is the asset of the welfare of society.

5. Test of reasonableness in relation with restriction under Article 19 (2) means application separately on account of consideration of impugned statute and no general standard would applicable as to all cases.

6. Court will decide reasonability on the basis of nature of right violated, purpose of restriction, degree and exigency of remedy search for, discrepancy of imposition and time condition.

7. It is not on the view of judges but on the basis of whether reasonable man will consider it as a reasonable or unreasonable the test of reasonability shall decide. Reasonability shall not be judged on the basis on the ground of restriction but on the ground of fundamental rights.

8. Whether law which is imposing restriction is reasonable or not decided on the basis of durability of a law, providing reasonable safeguards for rights like right to appeal or review.

9. The most important principle is that restriction on freedoms can be imposed only through by law or authority of law. it means that if state want to put reasonable restriction on the freedoms then legislation shall be passed by the legislature or under any existing law which limiting the freedom on account of social welfare.

10. Executive action or authority cannot impose restriction unless there is law behind to support and these restriction shall passed the reasonability test.

11. Restriction can be imposed only on the subjects listed in the Article 19 (2) and (6), not otherwise and if the reasonability challenged in the court of law then burden of proves will be in the shoulder of imposer has to prove it.

12. Arbitrarily imposing restriction will no e reasonable restriction, there must be direct and contiguous relationship between restriction and the object of imposing the restriction.

13. The principle of proportionality would be applicable between fundamental right and restriction court will decide on the basis of law imposing restrictions are

proportionate to the situation and it should be last chance to protect the welfare of society.

14. While deciding in the court of law reasonability based on procedural and substantive manner, it means law imposing restriction substantively sound under article 19(2) &(6) and procedural reasonability means restriction imposed under proper procedure law followed.

15. The object of restriction is very important; it means for personal gain or repugnance reasonability will not be cleared it is only for general profit of welfare reasonability test can be cleared.

RIGHT TO PRIVACY VS. CRIMINAL PROCEDURE

It is usual interpretation that no right is absolute and right to privacy is restricted according to the clause of Article 19 (2). So any law made by the parliament or existing may put the restriction on implementing the right available to the individuals under article 19(1), in the name of public order, security of the state, contempt of Court etc. Article 20(3) said that person is immune to provides witness and evidence against himself, no one can force to him. These are the fundamental right available against state so the responsibility of the state has incurs the liability to provide safeguards to enjoy this rights available under Constitution.

Also right to life is available under Article 21 of the Constitution, which is also limited by 'Procedure established by law'. Now the question is how far the provision of Criminal procedure Code is applicable in exercising fundamental rights of the Constitution. First we will discuss about criminal procedure about to give the compulsion for giving testimony. Now the interpretation may be extended in way of giving testimony including giving support to the Narco-analysis test.

Under section 2(h) defined that 'Investigation' means all the proceedings is conducted by police officer or any other authorized by Magistrate for the collection of evidence.

Section 53 of the Criminal Procedure Code, including explanation[243] added in 2005 shall read together to understand. Now so the investigating agency is allow under this section to conduct investigation, this is the narrow interpretation and so irrespective consent of the accused Narco-analysis test may be conducted with the virtue of this provision. So interpretation of 'such other tests' include Narco-analysis test. Such other test including (DNA test, blood sample test, and Narco-analysis test) find legal sanction through the adding explanation under section 53-A to Criminal procedure Code. Again in section 161 of Criminal Procedure Code, 'the police office is authorized for investigation and person is bound by the law to provide all the answer for the questions asked by him and it is bound by the law, excluding questions which tend to make him offender by law.[244] As general rule know to the legal fraternity that evidence collected through confession would not be considered as the evidence under section of the Evidence Act, 1872. Specific provision is available under section 25 of the same Act. Even though it is compulsory for person to give all oral answer it is not necessary that Narco-analysis test will be the compulsory, the crime which is registered under Indian Penal code shall be exempted for Narco-analysis test excluding terrorist activity.

CONDITIONS TO CONDUCT TEST

Informed consent: This is the prerequisite for conducting narco-analysis test otherwise it would be considered as compelled testimony under Article 20(3) of the Constitution. Informed consent means the person upon this test is conducted is aware about the mental and physical consequence and he is voluntarily agreed. He had the knowledge of the technicalities of the process, the influence of the drugs legal, physical, psychological consequences and voluntarily delivers the consent. Informed consent is the awareness

---

[243] R.V. KELKAR, "[Explanation.—In this section and in sections 53A and 54,— (a) 'examination' shall include the examination of blood, blood stains, semen, swabs in case of sexual offences, sputum and sweat, hair samples and finger nail clippings by the use of modern and scientific techniques including DNA profiling and such other tests which the registered medical practitioner thinks necessary in a particular case;" *Criminal Procedure Code* (Eastern Book Company).

[244] "The Code Of Criminal Procedure, 1973," *available at*: https://indiankanoon.org/doc/445276/ (last visited July 22, 2021).

of the accused or the patient procedure undergoing upon him. In Narco-test patient is aware about the consequences which may physical, legal and emotional. It is already explained to the patient or accused before undergoing treatment, in this test the doctor, advocate and physiologists presence is also important.[245]Accused during investigation cannot be subjected to Narco Analysis without his consent; it would be violative of Article 20(3) and 21 of the Constitution.[246]

Dr. D.Y. Chandrachud, J. in Justice K.S. Puttaswamy and others v. Union of India[247], A citizen has a right to safeguard the privacy of his home, his family, marriage, procreation, motherhood, child-bearing and education among other matters. Publication of any matter by anyone without individual consent whether it is appropriate or non-appropriate matter.[248]

In Nandini Satpathy case[249], Court declares that the accused not be interrogated without counsel present. The evidence supported before the court of law on the basis of the admission or confession even tough accepted but it the classic example most of the time incriminating evidence. Particularly when corroborated, as where the police have confirmed the accused disclosure of the hiding place of implements or fruits of the crime, In Nandini Satpathy case Supreme Court laid down the understanding of 'compelled testimony'. For compelled testimony not include physical force, threat or violence but psychological pressure, intimidatory methods, coercion and influence technique.[250] So this kind of technique amount to violation of Article 20(3) of the Constitution. The Supreme Court of India laid down following principles relating Article 20(3),

---

[245] Ananthi S. Bharadwaj and Sumithra Suresh, "Narco Analysis and Protecting the Rights of the Accused," 4 *NALSAR Student Law Review* 121–33 (2008).
[246] *Selvi v. State of Karnataka, AIR*, 2010, MCMLXXIV.
[247] *In K.S. Puttaswamy and Others v. Union of India, MANU*, 2017.
[248] *Ibid.*
[249] *Nandini Satpathy v. P.L. Dani and Ors., MANU*, 1978.
[250] *Ibid.*266

1. If an accused person desire to have his lawyer by his side when the police interrogate him, this facility shall not be denied to him.
2. The Police must invariably warn-and record the fact that writing any document amount to written acknowledgement
3. After an examination of the accused, where lawyer is not available, the police officer must take to the Magistrate, doctor or other willing person where he can unburdened himself beyond the view of the police.

JUDICIAL OPINION ON RIGHT TO PRIVACY

The judgment in Smt. Selvi v. State of Karnataka forceful or without consent of the subject if test was conducted then that would amount to violation of right to privacy of the individuals.

Any kind of force is not accepted in any legal format of the country, contaminated consent will be the denial and negation the justice. Justice is not only to be done it is necessary that actually all the principle of natural justice should have attached with the concept of justice. Justice K. Balkrishna said, the narco-analysis test would amount to violation of substantive due process. This is the most important recent decision on the right to privacy relation with narco-analysis test.

The guidelines given by NHRC in 2000 must be followed. It is also said by the court that consent given by the subject must be recorded before judicial magistrate. Statement registered under the authority of judicial magistrate would not be considered as confession but any further information received or material discovered from such can be admitted as a evidence before court.

In Justice K.S. Puttaswamy case [251], Supreme Court said, it is the government duty to upgrade its identity records in tune with changing requirements of the citizens.[252] From reasons purely personal to reasons flowing from life events such as marriage, death or migration, the authorities are responsive to the changing needs of citizens.[253] Supreme

[251] *Justice K.S. Puttaswamy and Ors. v. Respondent: Union of India (UOI) and Ors., MANU*, 2017.
[252] *Ibid.*
[253] *Ibid.*

Court held again, "it is bounden duty of all state instrumentalities to play the role of enablers in the exercise of rights by the citizens, including correcting their records owing to purely personal choices of the citizens. For instance, "gender" is an evolving concept which could warrant changes in identity documents. In such cases, too much insistence on disclosure of reasons could be invasive to privacy."

In a democracy, free expression of one's name in the manner he prefers is a facet of individual right. In Our Country, to have a name and to express the same in the manner he wishes, is certainly a part of right to freedom of speech and expression under Article 19 (1) (a) as well as a part of the right to liberty under Article 21 of the Constitution of India. State or its instrumentalities cannot stand in the way of use of any name preferred by an individual or for any change of name into one of his choice except to the extent prescribed under Article 19(2) or by a law which is just, fair and reasonable. Subject to the limited grounds of control and regulation of fraudulent or criminal activities or other valid causes, a bonafide claim for change of name in the records maintained by the Authorities ought to be allowed without hesitation.[254]

Recently in 2021Jigya yadav case[255] Supreme Court held, "The natural identity of an individual should be treated to be absolutely essential to his being. What nature gives is natural. That is called nature within. Thus, that part of the personality of a person has to be respected and not despised or looked down upon. The said inherent nature and the associated natural impulses in that regard are to be accepted. Non-acceptance of it by any societal norm or notion and punishment by law on some obsolete idea and idealism affects the kernel of the identity of an individual. Destruction of individual identity would tantamount to crushing of intrinsic dignity that cumulatively encapsulates the values of privacy, choice, freedom of speech and other expressions. It can be viewed from another angle. An individual in exercise of his choice may feel that he/she should be left alone but no one, and we mean, no one, should impose solitude on him/her."[256] Mental privacy of the individual is the essential part of life, Individual shall be treated discretely,

---

254 Rayaan Chawla v. University of Delhi and Ors., , DE/1983 MANU/ (2020).

255 *Jigya Yadav (Minor) through Gurdian/Father Hari Singh v. C.B.S.E. and Ors., MANU*, 2021.

256 *Ibid.*

his violation of own is detrimental to the humanity, it is the requirement of being as human and if there violation of individuality then that as will be treated as violation of very existence of man. Right to privacy is very personal to the individual even if god exist, shall not interfere into the individual jurisdiction. So without consent of individual any administration of drug will be treated as involuntary administration. This kind of narco or lie detector tests is an "intrusion" into a person's "mental privacy"

The consequences of such tests on "individuals from weaker sections of society who are unaware of their fundamental rights and unable to afford legal advice" can be devastating.[257]

It may involve future abuse, harassment and surveillance, even leakage of the video material to the Press for a "trial by media." Such tests are an affront to human dignity and liberty, and have long-lasting effects.[258]

"An individual's decision to make a statement is the product of a private choice and there should be no scope for any other individual to interfere with such autonomy."[259]

It has been held that when an order encroaches fundamental rights without due process of law it is still-born and liable to be ignored.[260]

In Hathrus Case [261] where Petitioner filed case in Allahabad High Court, petition no Crl. M.P. No. 105463 in 2020 Uttar Pradesh government take the decision to the conduct Narco analysis test of victim's family members to find out the truth. Girl was raped and died, Uttar Pradesh government to conduct Narco test was violation of the rule of law of the land.

NECESSARY GUIDELINES

1. The decision to decide whether Narco-analysis test shall be conducted or not decided by the High Court, now a days to conduct the Narco analysis the permission of

---

[257] Krishnadas Rajagopal, "Involuntary narco tests an intrusion into a person's mental privacy: Supreme Court" *The Hindu* (New Delhi, 4 October 2020), section National.

[258] "PressReader.com - Your favorite newspapers and magazines.," *available at*: https://www.pressreader.com/india/the-hindu/20201005/281998969913917 (last visited July 14, 2021).

[259] Right To Privacy – Civilsdaily, , https://www.civilsdaily.com/story/right-to-privacy/ (last visited Jul 14, 2021).

[260] *Jeeshan and Ors. v. State of U.P. and Ors., MANU*, 2021.

[261] *Satyama Dubey and Ors. v. Union of India, MANU*, 2020.

Trial Court is being taken because of it is the individuals fundamental right question, then High Court is the appropriate forum to decide. The informed consent of the person shall be cross verified by the High Court and if there will be absence of informed consent then High Court will reject the application and at the time of hearing the lawyer of the accused person shall be present and opportunity to disclaim shall be provided.

2. Narco-analysis shall be conducted in 'rarest of the rare' case, only because investigation agency not able to solve the case then be treating as last resort in investigation will be totally wrong in respective of the individual physical and mental health aspect. Even though this technique should not be treated as replacement for investigation method.

3. Narco analysis test shall be permitted only once in all investigation process and that also in only limited crime including terrorist activity or war against the state.

4. In vision of Supreme Court Judgement[262] in 2010 where Supreme Court has give order to strict adherence to the guidelines of National Human rights Commission in 2000, where including obtaining consent of subject it is mandatory to record video and it should be before judicial magistrate., consent form of the subject, signature of the subject lawyer, physical, explanation of legal and emotional consequences by lawyer and police and medical practitioner all going to be followed but after 20 years it has to passed new required guidelines because everything changed with the advent of time. Because in the name of these tests injustice may be done to the subjects if there is not ultimate discovery of truth in police case by the investigation officer.

5. Compulsory administration of Narco- analysis violates the "right against self-incrimination" and the test results cannot be admitted in evidence if they have been obtained through the use of compulsion but here is necessity that prosecution shall not be allowed to present the evidence has been collected from the information given by the subjects under Narco-analysis test. If any reference made by the prosecution during the trial then that may have to be considered as violation of Article 20(3).

---

[262] *Selvi v. State of Karnataka*, *AIR*, 2010, MCMLXXIV.

6. Guidelines given by the National Human Right Commission in 2000, and its adherence approved by the Supreme Court in 2010 does not satisfy the purpose, there is need for special legislation of at least Criminal Procedure Code amended Section 53 where 'such other test' is not conclusive, absence of informed consent procedure, so details and explanation shall be inserted in the section itself. There is necessity to add guidelines of Human Right Commission given in 2000, at least be incorporated under section 53 of CRPC.

7. In View of the Supreme Court decision the test results which conducted under section 161(2)[263] of the Code of Criminal Procedure, 1973 cannot be evidence taken through force. So section 161 shall add one more clause (4), any examination like lie detection, Narco- test or any DDT (deception detector techniques) shall not force by police officer without the permission of High Court.

CONCLUSION

Supreme Court of India time to time has passed through various judgements to concerning right to privacy as fundamental right, even though this fundamental rights are not absolute, still there is established process has to follow if state want to curtail or put the limitation on it, so it is necessary that law is very necessary to curtail the right to privacy but five times the bill was introduced to the parliament of India and that bill was not cleared by parliament.

As far as India is concerned, there is cynicism in the crime investigation methods applies by the police officers. In relation with right to privacy, Narco-test is not complement as it applied and conducted against any individuals without any legislation. Legal axiom is that whenever state wants to curtail the fundamental right or state wants to make

---

[263] "161. Examination of witnesses by police.",

Any person who have knowledge of the facts and circumstances

a) by a police officer making an investigation of the case: or
b) Police officer not below such rank as the state government may by order prescribed in this behalf.
c) Person whom calls to investigation is bound to give answer.
d) Writing down the statement by the police officer examination conducted under this section and making separate record of the each statement.

restriction on fundamental rights the proper legislation shall enacted but in relation with right to privacy no legislation passed till now by the government of India. The evidence collected through unfair means, if accepted in judicial proceedings raise disrespect towards the law. Narco-test in India is in the growing form not completely matured, absence of law, scarcity of rules and regulations is the actual plausibility of time. A person is entitled to wear fundamental right on account of social benefit and interest is relative question which can be solved by judiciary only but procedural safeguard which were laid down by the Supreme Court before a decade ago, not satisfied the purpose for which it was consigned. Law is the living course; it should be accommodate the living aspiration and desires of the people.

WHY GOD HAS NOT EVAPORATED?

DR. JAYKUMAR BHONGALE*

ABSTRACT:

During the last five thousand years, man has created many Gods. Peosple wasted their time and money to please their Gods. They believe that pleased God would bless them, and satisfy their wish and dreams, but God did nothing for them. In exchange for their worship, people face many social evil and diseases due to the dread of gods. These people are mentally slavering and enslaved by their priests. It may permissible for the ancient people, nomadic people out of their ignorance, they lived in darkness but today there is the light of science moves around the modern people, by virtue of science modern man is aware of each and every hidden mystery of nature, by virtue of science modern people need not worry about an unseen feature of demigod or unseen god. Man has found remedies for all the previous miseries of epidemic disease and famines. Modern man is seldom faced with mystery, misery, and helplessness. The ancestor of mankind had enough reason to imagine and worship the much more divine supremacy but the present generation has none. The concept of God may have to be lost its relevance today, because of literacy rate of the masses has been increased, and modern discoveries showed the exact truth of many hidden secrets which were prevalent in ancient society. Still, the prevalent subject is the persistence of the god delusion. Why do people still believe in the fabricated concept of god even after scientific advancement?

In the Present article, the researcher will point out the various reasons for the existence of God in the human mind even in the modern world where man believes in scientific answers to his problems. The researcher will try to point out the scientific and psychological reasons for the human mind converted into continued adherence to the reverence of God and religion. The researcher also makes some qualitative research through interviews and questionnaire responses got from the various respondents.

---

* Assistant Professor & Research Coordinator; Bharati Vidyapeeth Deemed to be University, New Law College, Pune.

INTRODUCTION

None has proved the existence of God; none has submitted any evidence for the existence of God. God is non-compatible with the developments of science and technology still god has been reverenced by the people. Reverence of God is definitely a personal issue of the individuals and the right to worship may consider a fundamental right like the right to religion available under Articles 25 to 28 of the Indian Constitution. This right to religion is available to all individuals situated around the world. The concern is not declining, demolishing, or criticizing the available right but the concern is about finding out the reason and motivation for the existence of God.

Today, devotees of almost all religions believe in modern science e.g. today Hindus have discarded a major section of the Vedas that describes magic and sacrifices to cure diseases. Modern Hindu priests did not chant hymns to heal patients, instead, they follow modern medicine. At the same time, Hindus continue to chant flattering hymns for gods from the same book. The same thing is applicable to the Christian and Jews, they do not follow remedies available in Bible, but they still worship the Bible. Uttering the hymns or teaching of the Bible does not cure the disease then how the bible or Vedas is being chanted or revered. Today all devotees believe in modern medicine but continue to revere their perceived gods. Why here doctrine of 'severability' is being applied as like being applied under Constitutional principles. According to this doctrine if any statute violates the basic core principle of the Constitutional Law then that statute would be declared as an ultra-virus to Constitution. It will be struck down by the Courts if it is challenged before the court. But this doctrine would be applicable where any part of the statute violates the principles of the Constitution then the whole statute would not be declared as a bad or ultra-virus but only that violating part if possible to remove, possible to remove means if after removing that violating part, the statute would remain active, independent and meaning of Statute would not be changed, from entire Statute.

There are some major reasons behind this fallacy of God and religion in this scientific time. There are four important pillars of the religion today;

1. Theory of Sins
2. Illiteracy and Poverty
3. Ancient Literature
4. Modern Priest

Without these pillars, it is not possible for religion to sustain itself in the modern era. The reasons in the modern era connected with the nature of man modern era have expanded, like the increasing ambition, coupled with their expectations of miracles and the limitation of science have helped to sustain the concept of God. People need a benevolent protector who actually fulfils their interests, expectation, and dreams. Man requires some saviour or patron protective figure, not necessarily actual or physical existence, imaginative or psychological protector is sufficient for harmed man. Without this support man's life is difficult, difficult to live, he wants to post responsibility for his misdeed or good work to someone else and that someone else will be always feasible. Any corner of the world whether it will in deep in the ocean or deep in the sky, whether in a spar-like dungeon or stroll in a forest. Many people get depressed without the support of some almighty power. The human desire for solace and comfort has led to the persistence of the most cherished illusion of mankind.

THEORY OF SINS

The foundation of the religion builds on the theory of sins, it means man's good deed and a bad deed will decide the pain and pleasure of an individual's life. What are the sins- it is the violation of God's rules, and what is the god's rules- the rules prescribed and developed under the religion, it includes the religious book, and its interpretations, rituals, rites, and most important the blessing of the priest. The priest is available to each and every religion through him only the door of heaven opened for the common people.

The true attraction of religion lies in its absolution or mercy. The sinner will be saved from the displeasure of life if he follows the true path of the god and the true path is the sole property right of the religion. Another path to diminishing the sin of the sinner is not permissible, unless and until the sinner will not chooses the right path propounded by religion he will not be free from transgression. This theory is the essence of all religions around the world and without this theory, religion would be a cadaver.

How this theory has been developed by man? Or did God himself come down to earth from heaven to tell the exact sense of ethics and morals? Even though sin and a good deed are deeply attached to ethics and morality still they are responsible to create this theory. Before the invention of agriculture condition of nomadic man was in the persecution stage, he could have easily become the prey of wild animals; he was subjected to hunger, wild animal, and weather. But the beginning of agriculture and socialization led to epidemic diseases, famines, poverty, exploitation, injustice, and crimes. Poverty led to poor hygiene, lack of adequate shelter, and food created ways for diseases and death. So the suffering of the individuals raised the question of their gods because the priest had maintained that God was a philanthropic entity and the well-being of the people was his prime concern. The human suffering laid the top of the question if some almighty and kind power had deliberately made the living being, why did he make the evils? The same kind of questions are available today if god is so kind then why did the rape-like incident happen to the innocent minor girls without their fault? Why do innocent people have to suffer and mighty people enjoy the fruits flourished by the feeble? To establish the concept of a kind and almighty god priests have to discover the cause of the evils. So priests evolved the concept that because of the sinners they are going to face these kinds of miseries. The dilemma of evil had always been a nightmare for all priests of all religions. So to maintain law and order with the help of the king made the social code of conduct was declared the rule of God or the divine word.

But again the question put forward that how an innocent baby can become a sinner? How do the weak people without fault become sinners?

ILLITERACY AND POVERTY

Illiteracy and poverty are also prime causes for the reverence of God. If you are weak or poor then lack of literacy is the root cause of your position. More you poor more you believe in the existence of God, because the god may provide you relief to sustain and to forget your pain and suffering. Not only individuals but also the whole society is inclined to provide solutions in the name of God to that suppressed individual. It is and was, the willingness of god to create a person to be poor and wear. Such kinds of averments prevailed and circulated in the society so, ultimately he tends to believe in the same premises which are available in the society and he hardly dared to challenge these premises because of a lack of real knowledge and education.

ANCIENT LITERATURE

Almost all the religions and their text were created in the name of God without any scientific investigation. The Vedas, Bible, Kuran, and all available religious books and literature promote the existence of God. According to all religious books, god is the ultimate, Ubiquitous but to prove this they did not provide any kind of evidence. And finally, it is mentioned that it is the belief of individuals who prove the existence and non-existence of God.

REASONS TO BELIEF AND NOT TO BELIEVE IN GOD

1. Believe that God has created the entire universe, all the reality of life, all human affairs controlled, and human morality supported and created by God.[264] It is not because it is mentioned in Dharmashatra or religious books, but where humans did not find an answer to the universe will connect with the concept of God.
2. The people who followed their own intuition in decision-making are not likely to believe in god.[265]
3. It is said that the more intelligent people are less likely to believe in God; because intelligent people are not dependent psychologically on the religious benefits. Intelligent people do not like to involve in religious bondage, so they feel more comfortable without the rituals

[264] Brett Mercier, Stephanie R. Kramer and Azim F. Shariff, "Belief in God: Why People Believe, and Why They Don't," 27 *Current Directions in Psychological Science* 263–8 (2018).
[265] *Ibid.*

of religion. These kinds of people try to find the answer out of the preview of religion. More religionists are more conformist toward the god.

4. It is been researched that people have a strong desire for self-enhancement, a positive approach towards life to achieve something great in life more persuaded towards the religion and god.
5. It is also being said that lonely people are less conversant about the belief in god but another research conducted by (Epiley, and Cacioppo, 2008) mentioned that more loneliness in life created more inclined toward the religion and god.
6. The existence of a deity who is simultaneously omnipotent and omnibenevolent is disputed by the problem of evil, which claims that such a god should not allow evil or suffering to exist.[266]
7. **Religious Psychological Prerequisites**

   Theory of Mind (TOM), the awareness that others' ideas, wants, and objectives influence people's behaviour. TOM enables complex social interactions and behaviour prediction in other people. Without it, you couldn't "place yourself in someone else's shoes."

   We are predisposed to accept religious habits because of our propensity to over-imitate. Humans acquire the majority of their actions and abilities from other people rather than via experience and trial and error. It is hard to solve problems on our own since the cultural knowledge that has been acquired over many generations is essential to our success. Additionally, some of this information runs counter to what you may infer based on your own observations or instincts.

   For instance, several civilizations have created strategies for preparing dangerous herbs (like Aboriginal Australians processing poisonous seeds of cycad plants).

   They have transmitted these ritualised practises without necessarily recognising the necessity of the challenging, drawn-out processes. But omitting what can seem like superfluous measures would harm you over time. Thus, imitating others can be advantageous for survival even when the motivations are hidden. If eminent people of your

[266] "Existence of God Definition, Arguments, & Facts Britannica," *available at*: https://www.britannica.com/topic/existence-of-God (last visited November 12, 2022).

community slaughtered deer every solstice, you definitely would too. This mindset is transferred to religious traditions.

The development of religions in human civilizations is probably a result of brain traits that have evolved over time, such as Theory of Mind and over-imitation. Natural evolutionary processes alone can explain why so many people believe in supernatural creatures.

RELIGION AND GOD

Religion and god are seemed to be connected in the usual fashion of understanding the people. Whether god has come first or religion? It is a similar question to whether the hen arrives first or the egg. The common belief among the society is that in-between man and god the religion has only performed the role of mediator, and conciliator. It also has the belief that religion is purely a personal matter between man and God. So, society has no role in interfering in the matter of individuals and every individual may be free to designate the faith and revere the god. Some researchers also argue also that if society has no role to interfere in the matter of worship of God then how religion is allowed to interfere in it? Another view is also important that to understand the function and purposes of religion it is necessary to separate religion from theology.[267] According to Dr. B.R. Ambedkar that the primary things in the religion were involved the usages, practices, and observances, rites and rituals and theology was secondary.[268] So, according to this premise, the primary purpose of religion was social. In the primitive society, religion was a medium relegated to life and preservation of life and it is these life processes that constitute the substance and source of the religion.

In today's society, God and religion are interdependent on each other, without religion there will be any reverence for the gods, and god worship is only possible through the entire jurisdiction of religion. In the present era between man and god not only the religion but one more mediator arrives and that is the modern priest. Without a modern priest, your worship of the god could not succeed even though you lived in a remote place

[267] Valerian Rodrigues, *The Essential Writings of Dr. B. R. Ambedkar* (Oxford University Press, 2002).
[268] *Ibid.*

in the country. He is available everywhere and in every religion. Without religion, there will not be god and without god, there is not any religion. Today god has the taken place of magic, superstition, and miracle. Without miracle and magic god will not be believed, he can do anything and everything.

ORIGIN OF RELIGION

Everything which affect them became a part of their religion. The ceremonies of the savage society were not only concerned with the events of birth, attaining manhood, puberty, marriage, sickness, death, and war but were also concerned with food. Among the pastoral people, the flocks and herds were sacred; among the agricultural peoples, seedtime and harvest are marked by ceremonies performed with some reference to the growth and preservation of the crops. Likewise drought, pestilence, and other strange irregular phenomena of nature occasion the performance of ceremonial. The life and preservation of life consist of the religion of the savage. What is true of the religion of the savage is true of all religions whenever they are found for the simple reason that constitutes the essence of religion. In a present-day society with its theological refinements, this essence of religion has become concealed from view and is even forgotten. But the life and preservation of life constitute the essence of religion even in the present-day society is beyond question. This was explained by Professor Crawley in these words,

"Man's religion does not enter into his professional or social hours, his scientific or artistic moments; practically its chief claims are settled on one day in the week from which ordinary worldly concerns are excluded. In fact, his life is in two parts; but the moiety with which religion is concerned is elemental. Serious thinking on the ultimate questions of life and death is, roughly speaking, the essence of his Sabbath; add to this is the habit of prayer, the giving of thanks at meals, and the subconscious feeling that birth and death, continuation and marriage are rightly solemnized by religion, while business and pleasure may possibly be consecrated, but only metaphorically or by the overflow of religious feeling."

THE DEVELOPMENT OF THE GOD-BELIEVING BRAIN IN HUMANS

The desire to believe in the paranormal is innate. Consider that 84 percent of the world's population, or close to 6 billion people, identify as religious, and that number is predicted to increase over the next several decades. 90 percent of adults in the United States, according to studies, believe in a higher power, spiritual force, or God. Atheists universally reject God, according to the same research, yet one in five acknowledge spiritual or higher powers.

Image 1.1 [269]

Size and Projected Growth of Major Religious Groups

	2010 POPULATION	% OF WORLD POPULATION IN 2010	PROJECTED 2050 POPULATION	% OF WORLD POPULATION IN 2050	POPULATION GROWTH 2010-2050
Christians	2,168,330,000	31.4%	2,918,070,000	31.4%	749,740,000
Muslims	1,599,700,000	23.2	2,761,480,000	29.7	1,161,780,000
Unaffiliated	1,131,150,000	16.4	1,230,340,000	13.2	99,190,000
Hindus	1,032,210,000	15.0	1,384,360,000	14.9	352,140,000
Buddhists	487,760,000	7.1	486,270,000	5.2	-1,490,000
Folk Religions	404,690,000	5.9	449,140,000	4.8	44,450,000
Other Religions	58,150,000	0.8	61,450,000	0.7	3,300,000
Jews	13,860,000	0.2	16,090,000	0.2	2,230,000
World total	**6,895,850,000**	**100.0**	**9,307,190,000**	**100.0**	**2,411,340,000**

Source: The Future of World Religions: Population Growth Projections, 2010-2050

PEW RESEARCH CENTER

In a nutshell, people tend to believe. This, according to evolutionary anthropologists, is no miracle. Evolutionary theory may be used to explain the beginnings and widespread nature of religious beliefs.

CONCLUSION:

In recent trends in world where people don't believe in God available under bible, Geeta or Kuran, but they believe in some other higher power or spiritual force of the Universe, and this number is increasing day by day. But this change happening only in countryside only where all facilities of education, freedom and liberty of thought and great livelihood available to the general people and other side where world facing from hunger, education,

[269] Benjamin Wormald, "The Future of World Religions: Population Growth Projections, 2010-2050" *Pew Research Center's Religion & Public Life Project*, 2015 *available at*: https://www.pewresearch.org/religion/2015/04/02/religious-projections-2010-2050/ (last visited April 3, 2023).

freedom and consistent persistent of subjugation available where more inclination and more constant adoption of primitive thought of firm believer of God.

After examining various perspectives on the question of why God has not evaporated, it is clear that the belief in God continues to hold significance for many people around the world. While the influence of religion may be waning in some societies, the search for spirituality and a higher power remains a fundamental aspect of human existence. Whether through traditional religious practices or alternative forms of spirituality, individuals continue to find meaning, purpose, and comfort in their connection to the divine. Ultimately, the persistence of belief in God suggests that, despite the challenges and uncertainties of the modern world, the human need for transcendence and a sense of meaning and purpose remains as strong as ever. The political system is briefly responsible to have more faith on God among the people, because religious people don't revolt against the present system that may be political, economic. So, it is better to have people concentrated on worship of the God rather than criticising the government policies and rule.

Witness protection in Contemporary legal world: mapping the criminal justice system

DR. JAYKUMAR BHONGALE*

MR. OISHIK BHATTACHARYA**

ABSTRACT

In spite of having one of the highest crime rates in the world, India is one of the few democratic countries in the world without a witness protection law. Due to the bureaucratic inefficiency the criminal justice system is suffering from sheer pain. The purpose of this article is to explain the situation of a witness in a criminal court. The various legal provisions that are somehow related to the witness's safety are given special attention in this paper by the researchers. The article also focuses on significant court precedents where the courts have attempted to offer some guidance to address the problem of witness protection. The article focuses on the potential use of video conferencing as a technique of witness protection. Without witness protection legislation, the courts have been forced to provide security and safety for the people who come forward to testify in court. In this paper, witness protection is largely discussed in terms of serious and organized crime. The purpose of this article is to examine shortcomings of India's current witness protection laws, their effects, and a comparative analysis of witness protection laws and programmes around the globe. This essay adopts a secondary research methodology and aims to contribute to the criminal justice system's need, to safeguard witnesses as well as pitching in ideas how India can also keep up with the global initiatives made in this field. In order to defend and sustain the idea of a fair trial, the author emphasizes the urgent need for independent laws for witness protection.

Keywords: Witness, Protection, Hostile, Fair Trial. Tribunal.

INTRODUCTION:

---

* Assistant Professor, Bharati Vidyapeeth Deemed to be University, New Law College Pune.

** Student of BBA LLB SEM VIII, Bharati Vidyapeeth Deemed to be University, New Law College Pune

A hearing without a free and fair trial would be violation the Article 21 of the Indian Constitution. The idea that justice must not only be done but also be perceived to have been done is well-established. A criminal justice system's main goals are to protect society from criminal activity, dissuade lawbreakers, and punish those who breach or seek to break the law. A thorough investigation is a key component of a criminal justice system that effectively prosecutes offenders. The process of evidence allows the adjudicating bodies to successfully contest or establish a fact by the methodical gathering and presenting of evidence in a court of law, in both civil and criminal issues. The evidence plays a major role in this investigative process. Documentary or oral evidence may be presented to the court or authority. The ability of the criminal justice system to work successfully depends largely on witnesses' willingness to share information and proof without being coerced or intimidated. Witnesses are in a difficult situation. The criminal justice system in our nation has failed, and witnesses are no longer willing to step forward and provide a statement. Witnesses are thought to be a class that has been deliberately ignored. The witness is helpless as he deals with the anger, intimidation, and pressure of the accused party, who also threatens his life and existence. When he learns that the state is not required by law to offer him security, the situation worsens.

The current study will concentrate on the function and status of witnesses in the Indian criminal justice system as well as the necessity for better witness protection among all of the supporting evidence. Oral testimony is typically provided by witnesses, including the accused, the victim, and anybody else with information about the case. In criminal trials, witnesses play a crucial role in the administration of justice by the court. Both documented and physical evidence are often submitted to the court through witnesses. They are the reason the trial uncovers some substance in order to get a just verdict. It is necessary that such a witness be shielded from the vengeance of extraneous elements that have the potential to alter his opinion regarding a particular case since the testimony of the witness may directly affect the conviction or acquittal of an accused. It is essential for the state to secure the security of such witnesses in order to maintain the predetermined path of justice. Extraneous circumstances like corruption or threats tend to make witnesses hostile.

In *Swaran Singh* v. *State of Punjab*[270], the Supreme Court of India expressed deep concern about the predicament of a witness in the following words: *"A criminal case is built on the edifice of evidence, evidence that is admissible in law. A witness in a criminal trial may come from a faroff place to find the case adjourned. He has to come to the Court many times and at what cost to his own-self and his family is not difficult to fathom. It has become more or less a fashion to have a criminal case adjourned again and again till the witness tires and he gives up. It is the game of unscrupulous lawyers to get adjournments for one excuse or the other till a witness is won over or is tired. There is no protection for him. In adjourning the matter without any valid cause a Court unwittingly becomes party to miscarriage of justice. A witness is then not treated with respect in the Court. He is pushed out from the crowded courtroom by the peon. He waits for the whole day and then he finds that the matter adjourned. He has no place to sit and no place even to have a glass of water. And when he does appear in Court, he is subjected to unchecked and prolonged examination and cross examination and finds himself in a hapless situation"*. For all these reasons a person abhors becoming a witness. It is the administration of justice that suffers. Then appropriate diet money for a witness is a far cry. Here again the process of harassment starts and he decides not to get the diet money at all.

WITNESS: UNDERSTANDING THE MEANING AND DEMARCATION

A witness is someone who was present at an event and can provide information about it, according to the common definition of the word. The term derives from the Old English word "witness," which originally meant "knowledge, wit". It signifies "attestation of fact, incident, and so on, from personal knowledge," as well as "one who therefore testifies." Being a witness is being there for significant occurrences or events. A witness is a person who can confirm crucial details about a crime or dramatic occurrence and has first-hand knowledge of it through their senses (such as seeing, hearing, smelling, or

[270] AIR 2000 SC 2017.

touching). In other terms, a witness is a person whose presence is required to establish the truth of a statement or occurrence. The Code of Criminal Procedure contains no definition of the word witness. The Indian Evidence Act does not directly define a witness either, but instead defines evidence in terms of just oral and written testimony under section. Oral evidence is any testimony that a witness is permitted or obligated to provide in court on a fact that is being investigated.

A witness is defined as "any individual, who possesses knowledge or documents regarding any offence" under section 2(k) of the Witness protection scheme of 2018 (the "Scheme").

The word "victim" has been added to Section 21's definition of CRPC, along with the phrase "guardians and legal heirs of the victim" (the victim is regarded as a key witness in a criminal prosecution).

THE RELEVANCE OF SAFEGUARDING WITNESSES IN THE CRIMINAL JUSTICE SYSTEM

New Testament of the Holy Bible teaches us: "Thou shalt do no murder, thou shalt not commit adultery, thou shalt not steal, and thou shalt not bear false witness." The importance of the witnesses to the trial process could be inferred from the words of an eminent thinker Jeremy Bentham: "witnesses are the eyes and ears of justice." The Hon'ble Supreme Court of India also held in *State of Gujrat* v. *Anirudh Singh*[271] that "It is the salutary duty of every witness who has the knowledge of the commission of the crime, to assist the State in giving evidence." Committee on Reforms of Criminal justice System said in its report that "By giving evidence relating to the commission of an offence, he performs a sacred duty of assisting the court to discover the truth. It is because of this reason that the witness either takes an oath in the name of God or solemnly affirms to speak the truth, the whole of the truth and nothing but truth".

In *Zahira Habibulla H. Shiekh and another* v. *State of Gujarat and others*[272]the definition for a fair trial was given as one "in which bias or prejudice for or against the accused, the witnesses, or the cause which is being tried is eliminated. If the witnesses get threatened

---

[271] (1997)6 SCC 514.

[272](2004) 4 SCC158.

or are forced to give false evidence that also would not result in a fair trial. The failure to hear material witnesses is certainly denial of fair trial."

The contradiction is that while criminals have a wide variety of rights (both constitutionally guaranteed and legally protected), victims and, more importantly, witnesses, have almost no legal protections. As a result of this unequal distribution of rights, witnesses are forced to become hostile because they lack the legal protections necessary to protect themselves.

In *Swaran Singh* v. *State of Punjab*[273], the Supreme Court made an observation, noting that one of the reasons someone would dislike testifying is because of the legal processes that are being followed.

THE CREDENTIALS OF THE WITNESS

A person who provides or is compelled by the court to provide evidence to the court is referred to as a witness. All other courts, forums, and judicial and quasi-judicial bodies accept evidence from witnesses. Three crucial issues come up when using the witness as a source of evidence.

According to section 118 of the Indian Evidence Act, "any person who is able to understand the question posed to them and is able to give rational answers based upon those questions."

i) Competency and qualification of witnesses;

ii) Liability of ensuring presence and testimony of witnesses in the court;

iii) The grounds for disqualification of the testimony.[274]

The evidence must be presented to the court in order to establish the facts. Competency and compellability are two different things when it comes to witnesses. A legally qualified witness must show evidence. The Indian Evidence Act of 1872's Section 118 addresses the credibility of witnesses. A prerequisite for testifying as a witness is one's competency.[275] Legal capability to present evidence in a court of law is referred to as

[273]AIR 2000 SC 2017.

[274]Dr B Yuvakumar Reddy, *Witness Protection in Criminal Trials in India*.

[275]Neha Singh, *WITNESS PROTECTION: A STEPPING STONE TO RESTORATIVE JUSTICE* (2022).

competence. It is argued that the witness does not have the right to testify if the judge may reject it due to legal requirements.

CONCEPT & REASON OF HOSTILE WITNESS

Hostile witness has not been defined in Indian law. A "hostile witness" is someone who refuses to disclose the truth at the instance of the party who has summoned him.[276] The 4th National Police Commission Report, noted that "prosecution witnesses are turning hostile because of pressure of accused and there is need of regulation to check manipulation of witnesses"[277] There are a number of additional reasons that contribute to the tendency of hostile witnesses. There are various reasons to turn hostile such as, it can be a fear of testifying against the defendant or criminal or political pressure from the government or family, or other societal factors. It's also feasible that financial incentives will influence witnesses. In recent years, incidences of witnesses becoming hostile during a trial as a result of threats have expanded beyond those involving grave offences like terrorist activities. Many techniques are used to discourage witnesses from testifying in front of the court and providing evidence. In recent years, incidences of witnesses becoming hostile during a trial as a result of threats have expanded beyond those involving grave offences like terrorist activities. Many techniques are used to discourage witnesses from testifying in front of the court and providing evidence. The trial breaks down when a witness retracts prior comments. When a witness makes a statement to police about committing an offence with his knowledge but then retracts it or modifies it when testifying in court during a trial, that witness is deemed hostile. A witness is considered hostile if he attempts to cover up the facts, harming the party who called him. That evidence need to be disregarded since it is unreliable. Any contradiction in a witness's testimony, however, cannot be used to counter the prosecution's case in and of itself.[278]

---

[276]James Fitzjames Stephen & 1829-1894 Sir, *A digest of the law of evidence*.
[277]4th Police Commission report.pdf, https://police.py.gov.in/Police%20Commission%20reports/4th%20Police%20Commission%20report.pdf (last visited Feb 22, 2023).
[278]*Atmaram & Ors.* v. *State of Madhya Pradesh,* (2012) 3 MLJ (Crl) 117 (SC).

There are several causes for hostile witness behaviour during a trial. Most of the time, accusers who are in positions of power or control are furious with the witnesses. Eighty witnesses in the infamous *Sidhartha Vashisht @ Manu Sharma* v. *State (NCT of Delhi)*[279] case had become hostile, leading to the lower court's acquittal—a decision that was later overturned by the higher courts. Apart from addressing the calibre and reliability of the evidence presented to the Court, the landmark ruling in the Zahira Habibulla case[280] ("Best Bakery") sheds light on the subject of witness protection.

The famous Sohrabuddin fake encounter case is also experiencing difficulties. A shocking 80 hostile witnesses were present.[281] Such obvious instances of hostile witnesses show the extreme side of influence and power in a nation where access to justice is already in a precarious position.

Such witnesses may be prosecuted under Section 191 of the Indian Criminal Code, which carries a seven-year prison sentence and a fine for those who provide false testimony. Perjury charges are, however, seldom brought.[282]

EVIDENTIARY VALUE OF STATEMENT GIVEN BY HOSTILE WITNESS

The evidence of a hostile witness cannot be discarded as a whole. In 2012, the Hon'ble Apex Court held that "the law can be summarized to the effect that the evidence of a hostile witness cannot be discarded as a whole, and relevant parts thereof which are admissible in law, can be used by the prosecution or the defence."

In *Balu Sonba Shindev* v. *State of Maharashtra*[283], the Supreme Court held that "the declaration of a witness to be hostile does not ipso facto reject the evidence. The portion of evidence being advantageous to the parties may be taken advantage of, but the Court should be extremely cautious in such acceptance."

---

[279]2001 Cri.L.J. 2404.

[280]Supra note 9.

[282]Sohrabuddin encounter: Number of hostile witnesses reaches 80- The New Indian Express, https://www.newindianexpress.com/nation/2018/jul/05/sohrabuddin-encounter-number-of-hostile-witnesses-reaches-80-1838857.html (last visited Feb 22, 2023).

[283]2003 SCC (Crl.) 92.

In *State of U.P* v. *Ramesh Prasad Misra*[284] , it was held that "it is equally settled law that the evidence of a hostile witness would be totally rejected if spoken in favour of the prosecution or the accused, but it can be subjected to close scrutiny and that portion of the evidence which is consistent with the case of the prosecution."

In *Basappa @ Basavaraj S/O Chandappa* v. *The State of Karnataka*[285], honourable Supreme Court of India observed that "In a criminal prosecution when a witness is cross-examined and contradicted with the leave of the court, by the party calling him, his evidence cannot, as a matter of law, be treated as Washed off the record altogether. It is for the Judge of fact to consider in each case whether as a result of such cross-examination and contradiction, the witness stands thoroughly discredited or can still be believed in regard to a part of his testimony. If the Judge finds that in the process, the credit of the witness has not been completely shaken, he may, after reading and considering the evidence of the witness, as a whole, with due caution and care, accept, in the light of the other evidence on the record, that part of his testimony which he finds to be creditworthy and act upon it."

WITNESS PROTECTION: A PERSPECTIVE FROM INTERNATIONAL CRIMINAL JUSTICE

In the form of various protective measures, the international criminal justice system recognizes that victims and witnesses are reluctant to testify before international tribunals. The witnesses are reluctant because they are afraid of being detained and prosecuted as well as of experiencing trauma after confronting the accused. Internationally, the necessity of establishing victim aid and witness protection measures has been acknowledged. International Criminal Tribunal for Yugoslavia ("ICTY") founded in 1993 has concurrent jurisdiction with the national courts in cases of egregious breaches of international humanitarian law.[286] The ICTY depends on international collaboration because support from the States is essential for advancing global justice. Successful investigation and evidence gathering are essential for carrying out its command in an efficient manner. The States' aid includes witness protection as well.

[284](1996) 10 SCC. 360.

[285](1999) 489 SCC. 544.

[286]Article 9 of Statute of the International Criminal Tribunal for Yugoslavia, 1993.

According to Article 21 of the ICTY Statute, the defence has the right to question each of its witnesses in the same way as the prosecution does. In accordance with Article 22, which addresses the protection of victims and witnesses, the Rules of Process and Evidence must include safeguards for the safety of victims and witnesses, in addition to requiring closed-door hearings and preserving witness confidentiality.

According to Rule 69, the prosecutor has the right to ask a judge to keep the name of any victim or witness who may be in danger secret until that person is under the protection of the Tribunal if there are extraordinary circumstances. The witness's name must be made public in a fair amount of time before the trial in order to prevent the defense's case from being jeopardized. A Trial Chamber is authorized by Rule 75 to take specific steps to prevent identity disclosure, including removing a victim's or witness's name and other crucial information from the Tribunal's public records, allowing testimony through closed-circuit television or in-camera proceedings to avoid confrontation with the accused, and managing the manner of questioning the victim or witness to avoid any intimidation.

WITNESS PROTECTION LAWS IN INDIA

A witness' civil duty is to tell only the truth when testifying in court. It is the responsibility of the State to safeguard a witness against dangers to his life or property in a variety of contexts. When a witness is intimidated, killed, or harassed, not only is the witness's life in danger, but also the citizen's fundamental right to a free trial is upheld.[287] Currently, there is no witness protection legislation in India. There are several statutes with provisions for victim aid and witness protection, but no single comprehensive law provides protection for witnesses.

Indian law divides witness protection into two categories, the first of which includes laws that contains some provisions, and the second of which deals with laws that are solely concerned with witness protection.

---

[287]Rutaganda - Judgement, http://hrlibrary.umn.edu/instree/ICTR/RUTAGANDA_ICTR-96-3/Rutaganda_Intro.htm (last visited Feb 23, 2023).

i) Anyone who tries to induce or influence a witness to give false evidence, is subject to a seven-year sentence under Section 195A of the Code of Criminal Procedure (Amendment) Act, 2008. This modification is a first step in the correct path. When sections 149 to 152 are read combined with section 148 of the Indian

Evidence Act, 1872, a witness is shielded from improper cross-examination, which is often necessary. The identity and address of witnesses must be protected under Section 16 of the Terrorist and Disruptive Activities (Prevention) Act, 1987. In-camera trials are also mentioned in the Act. S.17 of the National Investigation Agency Act of 2008, S.22 of the Unlawful Activities (Prevention) Amendment Act of 2004, the Criminal Law (Amendment) Act of 2005, and S.30 of the Prevention of Terrorism Act of 2002 have all addressed the issue. In the same manner Juvenile Justice (Acre and Protection of Children) Act, 2015, Whistle Blowers Protection Act, 2011, Protection of Children from Sexual Castes and Tribes (Prevention of Atrocities) Act, 1989 also contain provisions safeguarding the witness.

ii) In *Mahender Chawla* v. *Union of India*[288], the Supreme Court recognised the Witness Protection Scheme 2018 and declared that it will be "law" under Article 141/142 of the Constitution until competent legislation on the subject is enacted by Parliament or state legislature. Center, state and union territories shall enforce the same in letter in spirit.

WITNESS PROTECTION SCHEME, 2018

According to section 2(k) of the scheme "Witness means any person, who possess information or document about any offence."[289]

The "Competent Authority," which is defined as "a Standing Committee in each district chaired by the District and Sessions Judge with the Head of the Police in the district as Member and the Head of the Prosecution in the district as its Member Secretary," will be in charge of overseeing the programme.[290]

The phrase "Concealing of Identity of Witness" is defined in Section 2(b) of the scheme as "any condition prohibiting publication or revealing, in any manner, directly or

[288] 2018 SCC Online SC 2679.
[289] Witness protection scheme 2018(IND).
[290] *Ibid.*

indirectly, of the name, address and other particulars which may lead to the identification of the witness during the investigation, trial, and post-trial stage." The following are the scheme's main characteristics:

1) "An application for a protection order under the plan can be made in the appropriate form with supporting documentation with the Competent Authority of the District where the offence was committed through its Member Secretary."
2) When the Member Secretary of the Competent Authority receives an application in the prescribed form, it shall issue an order directing the Assistant Commissioner of Police (ACP) / Deputy Superintendent of Police (DSP) in charge of the concerned Police Sub-Division to submit a Threat Analysis Report.
3) Depending on the urgency of the situation due to an impending threat, the Competent Authority may issue interim protection orders for the witness or his family members while the application is on-going.
4) The Threat Analysis Report must be completed quickly and confidentially, and it must be delivered to the Competent Authority within five working days of receipt of the order.
5) The Threat Analysis Report will categorise the threat perception and advise protective steps to ensure the witness or his family is adequately protected.
6) While processing the application for witness protection, the Competent Authority shall communicate with the witness and/or his family members, employers, or any other person deemed fit, preferably in person and, if that is not possible, by electronic means, to determine the witness's protection needs. The Competent Authority will hold all hearings on witness protection applications in secret, maintaining complete confidentiality.
7) An application must be decided within five working days of the Police Authorities receiving the Threat Analysis Report.
8) The State's Witness Protection Cell or the Trial Court, as the case may be, will carry out the Competent Authority's Witness Protection Order. The State's Chief of Police will be responsible for the overall implementation of all witness protection orders issued by the Competent Authority. The Department of Home of the State, on the other hand, will

carry out the Competent Authority's Witness Protection Order for a change of identity and/or relocation.

9) After a Witness Protection Order is issued, the Witness Protection Cell is required to provide a monthly follow-up report to the Competent Authority.
10) If the Competent Authority determines that the Witness Protection Order needs to be revised or an application is filed in this regard, a new Threat Analysis Report will be requested from the Assistant Commissioner of Police (ACP)/Deputy Superintendent of Police (DSP) in charge of the concerned Police SubDivision after the trial is completed.
11) Part VI of the Gazette Notification states: "The State should give extensive publicity to this Scheme." Witnesses must be informed of the existence of the "Witness Protection Scheme" and its key characteristics by the I.O. and the Court.
12) There is also a provision for "Expense Recovery": "In the event that the witness has filed a false complaint, the concerned Government's Home Department may initiate proceedings for the recovery of the expenditure incurred from the Witness Protection Fund."
13) There is also a provision for "Review": "In the event that the witness or the police authorities are aggrieved by the Competent Authority's judgments, a review application may be filed within 15 days of the Competent Authority's passing of the orders." Due to the pressure from judiciary there are some witness protection laws and schemes under states level and it contain similar provisions as that of Witness Protection Scheme, 2018. Following are the schemes and legislation made by the state governments.

- Delhi Witness Protection Scheme, 2015
- Maharashtra Witness Protection and Security Act, 2017
- Odisha- Witness Protection Scheme, 2019
- Haryana Witness Protection Scheme, 2020

2018 WITNESS PROTECTION STATUTE HOLES

The 2018 witness protection programme has so many gaps. This is a summary of these gaps. This is a summary of these gaps:

• The recommendation made by the Mali math committee to establish an official to assist witnesses is not included, and there is no mechanism to preserve the witness's dignity.

• The provision of adequate facilities for the comfort of witnesses in the courtroom, such as chairs, relaxation areas, restrooms, drinking water, and so on, is not addressed in the plan.

• The plan does not include T.A. or DA provisions.

• The plan also did not address the problem of the case's postponement.

• There is no provision in the plan to prevent harassing witnesses.

COMPARISON OF WITNESS PROTECTION LAWS

Following years of advancement in the field of litigation practise, the testimony of a witness in a civil or criminal trial is highly valued and seen as crucial. The legal system would be hindered in the absence of this essential piece of evidence. Due to the lack of legislative protection for witnesses, it is becoming increasingly difficult to present reliable evidence from witnesses in criminal prosecutions.

UNITED KINGDOM

The Youth Criminal Justice and Evidence Act, 1999 (the "Act" or "YCJEA") was passed with the intention of modernising the criminal justice system against the backdrop of an inadequate and ineffective legal system that catered to the needs of distressed witnesses helping the court through their testimony. It aimed to improve the courts' capacity to address the unique requirements of witnesses who experience intimidation. By establishing particular measures to provide security and aid to the witnesses, the major goal is to enable the witnesses to give their testimony without fear and improve the quality of the evidence.

Three Sections, seven Chapters, and seven Schedules make up the framework of the Act. Part I covers the creation of referral panels, the orders directing minor offenders to appear before these panels, and the requirements for doing so. Nevertheless, this Section is no longer in effect.

The measures in Part II are designed to help the vulnerable witnesses provide testimony. The Act's Sections 16 and 17 specify the conditions for receiving aid. The possibility of delivering testimony[291]via a live link from a place outside the court, the capacity to testify in private[292], and the ability to conduct the chief and cross-examination via video recorded evidence are a few of the particular measures of protection. With regard to sexual offences, specific measures have been implemented.

CANADA

In order to maintain effective law enforcement and public safety, the Witness Protection Act of 1996 was passed. By helping a federal security, defence, or safety agency, the scope of protection is expanded to include those who are directly or indirectly involved in matters of law enforcement. Section 4 of the Witness Protection Act created the Witness Protection Program with the goal of providing protection as simple as possible. A witness is accepted into the protection programme under the terms of Section 5's provisions.

When deciding whether to accept a witness into the programme, a number of factors are to be taken into account, including the type or degree of risk the witness faces, the type of assistance given or agreed to by the witness, the witness's role in the matter, alternative options for protecting the witness, the viability of keeping the witness in the programme financially, and any other factors that are deemed relevant.

CONCLUSION

It is imperative to have a strong and effective witness protection statute in place to control and get rid of such unrelated elements that serve as obstacles to a fair trial. There are two aspects to the goal. From a trial perspective, the first concern is attempts to protect the investigation process and guarantee that witnesses do not retract

---

[291] Section 23 of the Youth Criminal Justice and Evidence Act 1999.

[292] Section 24 of the Youth Criminal Justice and Evidence Act 1999.

statements made in front of a judge. The second consideration is one of wellbeing of witnesses. Until the end of the trial, the witness has to be safeguarded from potential danger physically as well as emotionally. If we want to bring the criminals to the doors of Justice then witness's safety is important.

Efficient witness protection programmes are a crucial component of a whole criminal justice strategy to safeguard people who are essential to the dismantling of organised crime organisations. The following methods may be employed to develop an effective witness protection programme:

i) To assess the necessity to grant witness protection by the authorities in a fair and consistent manner, it is necessary to establish a comprehensive set of criteria or adopt common standards. These criteria could include the witness's role or importance in the case, the nature of the investigation, the nature of any threat to the witness' or his relative's safety, the results of the background check, the significance of the deposition in the case, and any other relevant or necessary criteria. This list is not all-inclusive. So, there should be Witness Protection Board in every District to implement above mentioned system.

ii) It is necessary to establish the reasons for ending the witness's protection. Protection must end if the protectee refuses to assist the authorities, falsifies papers, substantially misrepresents pertinent facts, or otherwise violates his or her obligations.

iii) Awareness raising programmes should be formulated targeting the criminal justice authorities (including judges, prosecutors, and police and prison officials) pertaining to witness protection in India.

LEGAL ENIGMA PIROUETTING SPACE TOURISM

DR. JAYKUMAR BHONGALE
MS. SAHELI CHAKRABORTY

Abstract:

Human interest these days has developed a particular inquisitiveness to unearth innovative objects, discovering the grounds in the wake of fables and superstitions, and now humanity's contemporary concern is the conundrums in outer space.

Owing to technological progress, now ordinary citizens can also visit space as a tourist and not just trained astronauts. Space tourism can be defined as exploring outer space for recreational, leisure and relaxation purposes.[1] India is at close quarters to securing a position for herself in the tillage of space tourism, question is; what are space tourism capabilities, and legal challenges for our nation?

KEYWORDS- Space law, Outer space, Airspace, Space tourism

Space tourism and India

Space tourism sometimes can be mentioned as citizen space exploration, personal spaceflight, or commercial human spaceflight, and it covers spaceflights that are sub-orbital, orbital, and even beyond Earth orbit.[2] For ensuring the harmonious and sustainable development of space tourism, appropriate laws are necessary. Space tourism is still a foreign concept and most of the people are unaware of this. Therefore when space tourism is launched and Indian civilians are ready for this new venture there should be accurate legal disclaimers and releases which the tourists need to sign to ensure that they themselves want to propel in space. Other factors like dispute settlement can also arise in outer space. Since space tourism is such a new venture, there will be multiple legal queries regarding this endeavour. Space tourism was a dream for Indians until today but it will now be possible. Today civilians wish to travel to space as a tourist, it is not foreign that they will not want to stay there for a vacation so legal angle of this should be vivid and be easily attainable.

While on one hand we are aware that facilities, infrastructure and space transportation network are significant elements of space tourism on the other hand governing laws should also be thought upon and discussed on.

India is party to an existing framework of the international law of outer space that, governs space tourism activities globally. There are five main multilateral treaties that have been finalised through the auspices of the United Nations Committee on the Peaceful Uses of Outer Space ("UNCOPUOS"), the main international body involved in the development of international space law.[3]

India's plan for space tourism

Previously in 2019, ISRO's chief K Sivan presented the features and proposed India's first space station for the first time. To utilise the best of India's space resources and increased space activities IN-SPACE was set up in June 2020. It is an independent and solo window nodal agency in the Department of Space for the advancement, encouragement and regulation of outer space activities of both government and private entities.[4] It can be said that this organisation hangs Indian Space Research Organisation (ISRO), and everybody who wants to take part in space-related activities, or use India's space resources together.[5] It is a demand driven model and so that it can help common citizens to experience space activities. Lately Union Minister of State, Jitendra Singh has disclosed ISRO has been carrying out a few viable studies for a sub-orbital space tourism mission on-board a liquid propellant stage booster. Gaganyaan is the first human spaceflight programme where three flights will be sent to orbit and will be two unnerved flights and one human spaceflight. Gaganyaan mission is the demonstration of human spaceflight's potential to Low earth orbit. What lies ahead are the missions which will be taken up subsequent to the triumph of Gaganyaan mission. Launching rockets, satellites and sending humans to space are two very different concept therefore the latter needs more expertise and has to be tested and tried before release. It is believed that 3-4 people will be sent to space for this purpose and as of now four Indian Air force officers are being trained for this mission who volunteered themselves to participate for the cause. Additionally, an escape unit have also been set up which aims intents to assist in difficult emergencies. Test of propulsion systems of the launch vehicle has been started and is going forward efficiently. Accomplishment of gaganyaan mission will lead to attainment of space stations. It is said that post the launch of gaganyaan mission within 5-7 years space stations will be brought forward. Santosh George Kulangara , from Kerala who is based in U.S happened to be the first Indian who travelled to space as a tourist.

ISRO has been planning for years for the development of low cost space tourism based on fair and inexpensive space technologies. Competence of ISRO is undoubtable since Chandrayaan and Mangalyaan missions were comparatively way low-priced than other countries who went down the same lane. Consequently it is believed that an inexpensive method of space tourism will be established.

Space tourism, which involves the travel of civilians to space for recreational, educational, or research purposes, is an emerging field that has gained significant attention in recent years. While several countries and private companies have been actively engaged in space tourism, India has also shown interest in this field and has taken steps towards its development.

ISRO (Indian Space Research Organisation), the national space agency of India, has expressed its plans to explore the potential of space tourism in the country. In 2018, ISRO announced that it was considering opening up its facilities for space tourism, including allowing private citizens to travel to space on board its spacecraft. ISRO has also sought proposals from the Indian industry for the development of space tourism-related technologies.

In June 2019, ISRO's then-Chairman, K. Sivan, stated that ISRO was working on a project to enable "space tourism in India in a big way" and that they were in the process of identifying suitable technologies and partners for the same. However, there has been no specific timeline or details on the progress of ISRO's space tourism plans since then.

In addition to ISRO, there are also some private companies in India that have expressed interest in space tourism. For example, a private aerospace company called TeamIndus, based in Bengaluru, has plans to launch a lunar rover to the moon as part of the Google

Lunar XPRIZE competition, and it has also expressed interest in offering lunar surface exploration experiences to tourists.

It's worth noting that space tourism is a complex field that involves significant technological, regulatory, safety, and financial considerations. The development of space tourism in India would require collaboration between various stakeholders, including government agencies, private companies, and international partners. As of now, space tourism in India is still in its early stages, and there are no operational space tourism programs available to the public. However, with the continued advancements in space technology and the evolving landscape of space tourism globally, it is possible that India may play a role in this emerging field in the future.

LEGAL OVERVIEW OF SPACE TOURISM IN INDIA

India ranks fifth in global space technology and is an exceptional accomplishment hence it cannot neglect space legislation. India has always had the view that all space associated activities is an international matter and to be a part of international laws and treaties are sufficient and adequate, hence the demand for a separate domestic law was not felt incumbent. Since there are no strong space laws in India, space tourism is a farfetched topic. India has made significant and substantial advancement into space sector over the years but regrettably still does not have a pertinent legislation. In view of these facts Department of Space had released Space Activities Bill in 2017. ISRO claims to launch its first space station by 2030 which is going to weigh 20 tons. Regulation of space activities were previously handled by ISRO and which is now handled by IN-SPACe, since it acts as a link between private organistaions and ISRO all of its decisions will be legally binding. National authorities grant consent for space tourism tuning with applicable legal provisions of air and space law. Also it is questionable that if passengers are to be treated as astronaut hence how their rights and obligations be defined. It is difficult to decide which legal regime will apply for space tourism i.e aviation/air law or space law.[7]

As of the knowledge cut-off date of September 2021, space tourism in India is a nascent and evolving field, and there are no specific laws or regulations that govern space tourism in the country. However, there are existing legal frameworks that are relevant to space activities in India, including space exploration and satellite launches.

The primary regulatory authority for space activities in India is the Indian Space Research Organisation (ISRO), which is the national space agency and responsible for the development and execution of India's space programs. ISRO operates under the Department of Space (DoS), which is part of the Government of India's Ministry of Space. ISRO has the authority to grant licenses and approvals for satellite launches and other space-related activities in India, and it sets the guidelines and regulations for these activities. ISRO's regulations include requirements for safety, security, and compliance with international space treaties and agreements to which India is a party, such as the Outer Space Treaty, Liability Convention, and Registration Convention.

In addition to ISRO's regulations, space tourism activities in India would also need to comply with other relevant laws and regulations, including those related to aviation, safety, liability, insurance, and environmental protection. For example, the Director General of Civil Aviation (DGCA) in India regulates civil aviation activities, and any space tourism activities involving manned spacecraft would likely require coordination and compliance with DGCA regulations.

It's worth noting that space tourism is a complex and rapidly evolving field, and the legal landscape related to space tourism in India may evolve as the industry progresses. As space tourism gains traction in India, there may be a need for additional laws, regulations, and guidelines specifically tailored to space tourism activities to ensure safety, security, and compliance with international obligations. It is important for stakeholders involved in space tourism activities in India to closely monitor the legal and regulatory developments in this area and seek legal advice as needed to ensure compliance with applicable laws and regulations.

At the moment, space related ventures and pursuits are legally governed by Constitution of India, 1950 which has provided due consideration for international law.

a) Article 51 provides state obligation to strive for promotion of international peace and security and [10]

b) Article 253 provides implementing the international treaties along with the domestic laws.[11]

DOS fundamentally promotes evolution and implementation of space science and technology for aiding extensive growth of the nation. Prior to its establishment, all of the space related activities were taken care of by Department of Atomic Energy.

What is Space Activities Bill 2017 and how is it a prospective legal backbone for space tourism?

The Space Activities Bill is legislation by ISRO in November 2017 which is meant to cover our nation's space goal meeting national and international obligations. The key propositions of this bill includes that it shall be applicable to all citizens of India, a non-transferable licence will be provided to any person carrying out any space commercial activity by the government, ensure safety requirements and supervise conduct and provide technical and professional support for commercial space activities.[8] As reported by Department of Space at present government has said, there are no laws capable to govern space tourism and there are almost no plans to make a law specific to space tourism in our country. [9] India is one of the members to the Outer Space Treaty, 1967. The Constitution of India administers for implementation of international treaty obligations in Articles 51 and 253. Since there was a lack of domestic participation of India and a vacancy of pertinent legislative framework, Government of India as a welcome step with suggestions from the public has drafted Space Activities Bill 2017 to frame clearer laws in developing the space sector with an objective to regulate space activities in India. The implementation of this bill will surely be a breakthrough for space companies but sadly it has not yet been approved and therefore is not a legally binding document. There lies a definite question of law on disputes arising in outer space. This Bill being passed will enhance our nation's interests. Also as an inheritor to the Satcom Policy , the Indian Space Research Organisation (ISRO) also have given birth to a new Spacecom Policy 2020 to carry out the commercial use of orbital slots, satellites, and ground stations for communication needs. This policy is also the cause for the formulation of Indian National Space Promotion & Authorization Center (IN-SPACe).

As of the knowledge cut-off date of September 2021, space tourism in India faces several challenges and difficulties, including:

Regulatory Framework: There is no specific legal framework or regulations governing space tourism in India. Existing regulations by the Indian Space Research Organisation (ISRO) primarily focus on satellite launches and other space-related activities, and there are no specific guidelines or regulations that specifically address the unique aspects of space tourism.

Licensing and Approval Process: Obtaining licenses and approvals for space tourism activities in India can be complex and time-consuming. ISRO, as the regulatory authority for space activities in India, may require thorough safety, security, and compliance assessments, which can pose challenges for space tourism operators in terms of compliance, documentation, and coordination.

Infrastructure and Technology: Building the necessary infrastructure and technology for space tourism in India requires significant investments, including launch facilities, spacecraft, and supporting systems. Developing such infrastructure and technology can be expensive and may pose challenges in terms of funding, technological expertise, and capabilities.

Safety and Security: Space tourism involves inherent risks, including those associated with human spaceflight, spacecraft operations, and space environment. Ensuring the safety and security of space tourists is a critical challenge, including measures to mitigate risks, emergency preparedness, and contingency planning.

Liability and Insurance: The issue of liability and insurance for space tourism activities is complex and can pose challenges. Determining liability in case of accidents or damages during space tourism activities, and obtaining appropriate insurance coverage for potential risks, including third-party liability and property damages, can be challenging.

Public Perception and Acceptance: Space tourism is a novel concept in India, and public perception and acceptance of this industry may pose challenges. Cultural, ethical, and social considerations, as well as concerns related to environmental impacts, could impact the acceptance and growth of space tourism in India.

International Obligations: India is a signatory to several international treaties and agreements related to space, including the Outer Space Treaty, Liability Convention, and Registration Convention. Complying with these international obligations, including issues related to liability, property rights, and registration of space objects, can pose challenges in the context of space tourism.

It's important to note that the challenges and difficulties of space tourism in India are not unique to the country and are similar to those faced by the space tourism industry globally. As space tourism continues to develop and evolve, addressing these challenges will require coordination among stakeholders, regulatory frameworks, investments in infrastructure and technology, safety and security measures, public outreach, and compliance with international obligations.

NASA

In the U.S., the licensing and approval process for space tourism activities, including those involving NASA, is governed by the Federal Aviation Administration (FAA) and the Commercial Space Launch Act (CSLA). The FAA's Office of Commercial Space Transportation (AST) is responsible for regulating and licensing commercial space launches and re-entries, including those for space tourism purposes, in accordance with the CSLA.

The licensing and approval process for space tourism activities in the U.S., including those involving NASA, typically involves the following steps:

Licensing and Permitting: Companies or organizations planning to conduct space tourism activities must obtain licenses or permits from the FAA's Office of Commercial Space Transportation (AST) for space launches, re-entries, or other commercial space activities. These licenses or permits are typically issued after thorough reviews of safety plans, technical specifications, and other relevant documentation.

Compliance with Safety Regulations: Space tourism operators are required to comply with various safety regulations, guidelines, and standards established by the FAA, NASA, and other relevant agencies. These may include requirements related to spacecraft design, systems, operations, crew training, emergency preparedness, and risk mitigation.

Environmental Assessments: Space tourism operators may need to conduct environmental assessments and obtain approvals or permits for potential environmental impacts associated with their activities, such as launch emissions, noise, and other environmental considerations.

Coordination with NASA: Space tourism operators may need to coordinate with NASA for various aspects of their activities, including launch facilities, spacecraft integration, payload accommodations, safety reviews, and other collaborations or partnerships.

Insurance and Liability: Space tourism operators are typically required to obtain appropriate insurance coverage to address potential risks and liabilities associated with their activities, including third-party liability and property damages.

It's important to note that the licensing and approval process for space tourism activities, including those involving NASA, can be complex and may require compliance with multiple regulations, guidelines, and standards. The specific requirements may vary depending on the nature, scope, and location of the space tourism activities, as well as the involvement of NASA or other relevant agencies. It's advisable to consult with legal and regulatory experts familiar with the relevant laws and regulations when considering or engaging in space tourism activities.

RUSSIA

The Russian Federal Space Agency, commonly known as Roscosmos, is the government body responsible for the space science program of the Russian Federation and general aerospace research. Roscosmos plays a significant role in space tourism, as it is responsible for managing and coordinating various space activities, including those related to space tourism.

Roscosmos has been involved in space tourism through its partnership with Space Adventures, a private space tourism company based in the United States. Roscosmos has facilitated several space tourism missions to the International Space Station (ISS) using Russian spacecraft, including Soyuz capsules, which have carried private individuals as space tourists.

PRIVATE COMPANIES AND SPACE TOURISM

Private companies and space tourism have been gaining significant attention in recent years as the accessibility of space exploration has expanded beyond just government agencies. Several private companies are now actively involved in developing spacecraft and offering space tourism experiences to the public. Here are some key points about private companies and space tourism:

Space Tourism: Private companies like SpaceX, Blue Origin, and Virgin Galactic are at the forefront of the emerging space tourism industry. They are developing spacecraft that can carry civilians to space for recreational and tourism purposes. These companies have ambitious plans to offer suborbital and orbital space tourism experiences, where civilians can experience weightlessness, see Earth from space, and even visit other celestial bodies like the Moon.

Technological Advancements: Private companies have been driving technological advancements in the space industry, including the development of reusable rockets and spacecraft. SpaceX, for example, has successfully launched and landed reusable rockets, significantly reducing the cost of accessing space. This has paved the way for more affordable space tourism options, making it more accessible to a broader range of people.

Market Potential: Private companies see a huge market potential in space tourism, with projections of a multi-billion dollar industry in the coming years. There is a growing interest among affluent individuals and corporations to experience space travel, which has fueled investments in private space tourism ventures. Companies like Blue Origin and Virgin Galactic have already started taking reservations for space tourism flights, with tickets priced in the hundreds of thousands to millions of dollars.

Research and Development: Private companies involved in space tourism are not just focused on recreational trips to space, but also on conducting research and development activities. These companies are collaborating with scientists, researchers, and institutions to conduct experiments, test technologies, and gather data in microgravity environments, which can have applications in various fields such as medicine, materials science, and agriculture.

Regulatory Challenges: Private companies involved in space tourism are facing regulatory challenges as space is governed by various international treaties, agreements, and laws. Issues related to safety, liability, insurance, and environmental impact are some of the key regulatory challenges that need to be addressed. Governments and space agencies are working on regulations to ensure the safety of space tourism activities while promoting responsible and sustainable space exploration.

Public Interest and Ethical Considerations: The emergence of private companies in space tourism has also raised ethical considerations and concerns about equity and access. Critics argue that space tourism is currently limited to the ultra-rich and that it exacerbates social and economic inequalities. There are also concerns about the impact of space tourism on the environment and the potential exploitation of celestial bodies. These issues are being debated and discussed by various stakeholders, including governments, space agencies, private companies, and the public.

Iprivate companies are playing a significant role in the development of the space tourism industry, making space exploration more accessible and commercially viable. While there are many opportunities associated with private companies and space tourism, there are also challenges that need to be addressed to ensure responsible and sustainable space exploration in the future.

Private ventures in space tourism face several challenges, including:

High Costs: Developing space tourism infrastructure, including spacecraft and launch systems, is extremely expensive. The costs associated with research and development, manufacturing, testing, and launching spacecraft can be prohibitive for private companies, especially startups or small ventures. The need to invest substantial capital in developing cutting-edge technology and infrastructure poses a significant challenge for private companies in space tourism.

Regulatory Hurdles: Space is governed by various international treaties, agreements, and laws, which can pose regulatory challenges for private space tourism ventures. Obtaining necessary licenses, permits, and approvals from government agencies can be complex and time-consuming. There are also safety regulations, liability issues, and environmental concerns that need to be addressed, which can pose legal and regulatory challenges for private companies.

Safety and Liability Concerns: Space tourism involves inherent risks, including the health and safety of passengers during launch, re-entry, and space travel. Ensuring the safety of passengers and addressing liability issues in case of accidents or mishaps can be a significant challenge for private companies. Adequate insurance coverage, risk mitigation strategies, and compliance with safety standards are essential, but can be costly and complex.

Technical and Operational Complexities: Developing spacecraft and launch systems for space tourism requires cutting-edge technology, expertise in aerospace engineering, and operational capabilities. Private companies need to invest in research and development, testing, and operational capabilities, which can pose technical and operational challenges. Maintaining and operating spacecraft, managing logistics, and ensuring reliable and safe operations in the harsh environment of space are complex tasks that private companies must navigate.

Market Viability and Competition: The market demand for space tourism is still uncertain, and the competition among private companies in the emerging space tourism industry is increasing. Companies need to develop viable business models, attract customers, and generate sufficient revenue to sustain their operations. Market uncertainties, competitive pressures, and changing customer preferences can pose challenges for private companies to establish a sustainable business in the space tourism market.

Ethical and Social Concerns: The emergence of space tourism has raised ethical and social concerns, including issues related to equity, access, environmental impact, and exploitation of celestial bodies. Private companies need to address these concerns, comply with ethical standards, and demonstrate responsible practices in their operations. Balancing commercial interests with ethical and social considerations can be a challenge for private companies in the space tourism industry.

Dependence on Government Support: Private companies in space tourism often rely on government contracts, partnerships, and support for funding, regulatory approvals, and infrastructure access. Changes in government policies, funding availability, or geopolitical dynamics can pose challenges for private companies, as they may impact their business operations, partnerships, and access to resources.

While private companies are driving innovation and advancement in the space tourism industry, they face significant challenges including high costs, regulatory hurdles, safety and liability concerns, technical complexities, market viability, ethical considerations, and dependence on government support. Overcoming these challenges requires strategic planning, technological expertise, operational capabilities, compliance with regulations, and responsible business practices.

LIABILITY IN SPACE TOURISM

Liability refers to the legal responsibility or obligation for damages or losses that may arise from space tourism activities. In the context of space tourism, liability can arise from various sources, such as accidents during space launches or landings, in-flight incidents, collisions with space debris or other objects, damage to third-party property, injuries to passengers or crew, and other unforeseen events.

Insurance, on the other hand, involves transferring the risks associated with space tourism activities to an insurance provider through a contractual agreement. Space tourism operators and other stakeholders, such as launch service providers, spacecraft manufacturers, and spaceports, typically obtain various types of insurance coverage to protect themselves financially against potential liabilities and losses.

Liability and insurance clauses in space tourism typically cover a range of aspects, including:

Third-party liability: This involves liability for damages or losses to third parties, such as passengers, crew, other spacecraft, property, or the environment.

Property damage: This involves coverage for damage or loss of spacecraft, launch vehicles, or other property used in space tourism activities.

Personal injury: This involves coverage for injuries or fatalities to passengers, crew, or other individuals involved in space tourism activities.

Collision and debris mitigation: This involves coverage for damages resulting from collisions with space debris or other objects in space and costs associated with debris mitigation measures.

Product liability: This involves coverage for damages resulting from defects or failures of spacecraft, launch vehicles, or other products used in space tourism activities.

Business interruption: This involves coverage for losses resulting from disruptions to space tourism operations due to unexpected events, such as accidents, technical failures, or regulatory issues.

Worker's compensation: This involves coverage for injuries or illnesses to workers involved in space tourism activities.

Liability and insurance requirements for space tourism activities vary depending on the jurisdiction, type of activity, and parties involved. Some countries or international organizations may have specific regulations or guidelines related to liability and insurance for space tourism, and space tourism operators may be required to obtain certain minimum levels of coverage or demonstrate financial responsibility.

Space tourism operators and stakeholders typically work with insurance providers specializing in space or aviation insurance to obtain appropriate coverage for their activities. The terms, conditions, and coverage of liability and insurance clauses in space tourism contracts are typically negotiated and customized based on the specific circumstances and risks associated with the space tourism activity.

It's important for space tourism operators and stakeholders to carefully review and understand the liability and insurance requirements, and work with experienced legal and insurance professionals to ensure that appropriate coverage is in place to protect against potential risks and liabilities associated with space tourism activities.

The liability clause in space tourism is governed by a combination of national and international laws, regulations, and conventions, depending on the jurisdiction and location of the space tourism activity. Here are some specific laws and regulations that may be relevant to the liability clause in space tourism:

International Treaties: There are several international treaties that govern space activities, including space tourism, and may include provisions related to liability. The most important treaty in this regard is the Outer Space Treaty, also known as the Treaty on Principles Governing the Activities of States in the Exploration and Use of Outer Space, including the Moon and Other Celestial Bodies, which sets out the fundamental principles of space law, including liability for damages caused by space objects. Other relevant treaties include the Liability Convention and the Registration Convention, which also address liability issues in space activities.

National Space Laws: Many countries have their own national laws and regulations related to space activities, including space tourism. These laws may include provisions related to liability, insurance, and compensation for damages arising from space tourism activities. For example, in the United States, the Commercial Space Launch Act and its implementing regulations provide for liability and insurance requirements for commercial space launches, including space tourism activities.

Launch Licensing and Permitting Regulations: Space tourism operators may be required to obtain licenses or permits from national or regional space authorities for conducting space tourism activities. These licensing or permitting regulations may include provisions related to liability, insurance, and indemnification requirements for space tourism operators.

Contractual Agreements: Liability clauses in space tourism contracts are typically customized and negotiated between the parties involved in the space tourism activity, including the space tourism operator, passengers, and other stakeholders. These contractual agreements may include provisions related to liability, insurance, indemnification, and dispute resolution mechanisms.

Insurance Requirements: Space tourism operators may be required to obtain liability insurance coverage to mitigate potential risks and liabilities associated with space tourism activities. Insurance requirements may be imposed by national or regional space authorities, or may be included as part of contractual agreements between the parties involved in space tourism activities.

It's important to note that the legal landscape related to space tourism and liability is still evolving and may vary depending on the jurisdiction and location of the space tourism activity. It's recommended for space tourism operators and stakeholders to work with experienced legal professionals and consult applicable laws, regulations, and conventions to ensure compliance with the relevant legal requirements and to properly address liability issues in space tourism activities.

Space tourism and Environment

Space tourism, like any other human activity, has the potential to impact the environment. Some of the potential environmental impacts of space tourism include:

Atmospheric Pollution: Space launches, especially those using traditional rocket propulsion systems, can release various gases and particulate matter into the atmosphere, contributing to air pollution. Emissions from rocket engines can release greenhouse gases, such as carbon dioxide and water vapor, as well as other pollutants, such as nitrogen oxides and soot, which can contribute to the formation of smog and other air quality issues.

Noise Pollution: Space launches generate high levels of noise, which can have impacts on wildlife, ecosystems, and nearby communities. The loud noise from rocket launches can disturb wildlife habitats, disrupt sensitive ecosystems, and affect local communities' quality of life.

Space Debris: Space tourism activities can contribute to the accumulation of space debris or space junk, which consists of defunct satellites, spent rocket stages, and other debris from space missions. Space debris can pose risks to operational satellites, spacecraft, and the International Space Station (ISS), as well as create potential hazards for future space missions.

Visual and Light Pollution: Space tourism activities, including those involving space tourism vehicles or spaceports, can introduce additional lights and structures into the night sky, potentially affecting natural dark skies, stargazing, and astronomical observations.

Ecological and Cultural Impacts: Space tourism activities, such as construction of spaceports, launch facilities, or infrastructure, can have ecological impacts, such as habitat destruction, disruption of local ecosystems, and impacts on local cultural heritage and traditional practices.

Resource Utilization: Space tourism activities, such as space mining or resource extraction, could potentially impact natural resources in space, such as minerals, water, and other materials, which may have ecological, legal, and ethical implications.

It's important to note that space tourism is still a relatively nascent industry, and the full extent of its potential environmental impacts is not yet fully understood. However, there is increasing recognition and efforts to address and mitigate these impacts through environmental regulations, guidelines, and best practices, as well as technological innovations and sustainable practices in the design and operation of space tourism vehicles and infrastructure.

As space tourism continues to develop, it will be essential to ensure that environmental considerations are carefully addressed to minimize negative impacts and promote sustainable practices in this emerging industry.

CONCLUSION

India has to reach a level where in the legal status of everyone involved in space tourism is successfully defined starting from commanders, crew members to passengers. It is recommended that India should have efficient, robust and appropriate space laws which will facilitate space tourism in India. Relying on International Treaties will not be enough to cover all aspects of space law especially in the field of space tourism which is lucrative but highly competitive as well. At India International Science Festival (IISF) 2023, Dr. S. Somanath, Chairman of the Indian Space Research Organisation (ISRO) did speak about avenues space tourism and the development of reusable rockets which is a ray of sunshine to our hope for space tourism. If India wishes to secure a competitive spot in space market, she will need a comprehensive space law on tourism which will lead to a generous revenue for companies that will provide the facility. Hence, it will also be a pathway for an increase in employment. It is predicted that India will make space tourism possible by 2030 but whether India will develop a strong legislation regarding space laws remains to be seen.

References

[1] Failat YA, "Space Tourism: A Synopsis on Its Legal Challenges" Ir. Law J., https://www.academia.edu/2348919/Space_Tourism_A_Synopsis_on_its_Legal_Challenges viewed 28 February 2023.

[2] https://www.revfine.com/space-tourism/#what-is-space-tourism

[3] Freeland S, "Up, up and ... Back: The Emergence of Space Tourism and Its Impact on the International Law of Outer Space" (2005) 6 Chic. J. Int. Law 1, https://heinonline.org/HOL/Page?handle=hein.journals/cjil6&id=9&div=&collection=.

[4] "What Is IN-SPACe? - Civilsdaily", https://www.civilsdaily.com/news/what-is-in-space/ viewed 3 March 2023.

[5] "INSPACe- Optimize IAS", https://optimizeias.com/inspace/ viewed 3 March 2023.

[6] Shairwal SLA-S, Legal Overview of Space Law in India (6 December 2021) Lexology, https://www.lexology.com/library/detail.aspx?g=4d90359c-b79e-40c3-8d2c-8c9fdf308484 viewed 3 March 2023.

[7] Hobe PS, "Legal Aspects of Space Tourism" 86 Neb. LAW Rev.

[8] Space Activities Bill | Simplified UPSC (1 August 2021), https://simplifiedupsc.in/space-activities-bill/ viewed 15 March 2023.

[9] Government Says, at Present There Are No Laws Governing Space Tourism in the Country and There Are No Plans to Make a Law Specific to Space Tourism,

https://pib.gov.in/pib.gov.in/Pressreleaseshare.aspx?PRID=1845769 viewed 5 March 2023.

[10] Constitution of India, https://www.constitutionofindia.net/constitution_of_india/directive_principles_of_state_policy/articles/Article%2051 viewed 15 March 2023.

[11] Constitution of India, https://www.constitutionofindia.net/constitution_of_india/relations_between_the_union_and_the_states/articles/Article%20253 viewed 15 March 2023.

POST-RETIREMENTS RECRUITMENTS OF JUDGES, JUDICIAL RECUSAL AND JUDICIAL ACCOUNTABILITY

MR. JAY KUMAR BHONGALE

Abstract: Indian Constitutional law is silent about the post retirements assignments of the higher court judges. Appointments of judges and judicial accountability has close connection between these two variables, if appointments have been carried out not on the basis of merit or caliber but it was carried out on the basis of political connection then definitely there would be violation of rule of law and mannerisms of judicial accountability. In India, it is a regular phenomenon that retired judges of the Supreme Court and High Court are appointed to some assignments by the government. So, this is a major issue in the Indian judicial system that postretirement assignments carried out with political intention and benefits which also affect delivery of administration of justice, judges give favorable judgements in favour of the political parties on account of future lucrative assignments.

In Present article researchers will discuss this issue in detail on the basis of non-empirical data. Non-empirical data will include law commission reports, the Supreme Court judgements, constitutional principles, general principles of judicial conduct and international standards for judges. Judicial accountability is getting injured because of the post-retirement assignments of the Superior court judges. Researchers will try to prove this hypothesis in this article.

Keywords: Judicial Accountability, post-retirement assignments, Colleguim, miscarriage of justice, civil liberties.

Introduction:

Judicial accountability is getting injured because of the post-retirement assignments of the Superior court judges. This premise is toughly applicable to the present Indian Judicial system. This fact is undeletable even though the Indian Judiciary is the strongest judiciary in the world. Indian Judiciary is the champion of the fundamental rights of the Individuals. The retiring judges of the Supreme Court and High Courts pronounced the judgements which will be pleased the government to gain the post-retirement appointment like various tribunals and commissions.

"The behavior of judges is closely scrutinized to ensure continued confidence in the integrity of the courts".[1] The public confidence will evaporate if judges seem to be biased when it happens then very institution of Judiciary will lost its worth and the whole judicial function difficult to exercise.[2] Therefore, action which is connected with self-interest and preconception, Judges shall be deserted from it. It was mentioned by author that, "Throughout the ages, and in all societies, impartiality has been regarded as the essence of the administration of justice. It is essential for a judge to maintain, in court, a demeanor which gives to the parties an assurance that their case will be heard and determined on its merits, and not according to some personal predisposition on the part of the judge".[3]Judges and normal citizens are similar according to physical appearance but mentally and emotionally they have to be differing from them. It is expressed by author that, "The Judges, also human beings, do not approach the task of adjudication blindfolded. They disembark at the bench already fashioned by their own experiences and by the perception of the society they come from, and they might have belief and disbelief, like everyone else. The difference may happen between judicial fairness and the human being nature of judges. Judges shall not deny their human nature relatively; they have to acknowledge it".[4] But when they accept their human nature "they shall be in position to recognize how they can reach impartiality which is demand of their job".[5]

"The Constitution vests a lot of power and a certain amount of immunity in judges. Fairness and impartiality are the fundamental qualities to be possessed by a judge. In India, for the vast majority of cases, there are no reports of having been heard by a partial and unfair judge but there are instances where the contrary happens".[6]

It was held in *Ram Jawaya* v. *State of Punjab*[7] that in India, and Indian Constitution has not completely accepted the theory of separation of power in rigid sense even though role of branches of the government has adequately separated from each other because Indian constitution believes that, "One organ of the government shall not interfere and function of other branch of the government".[8]

Independence of judges does not mean independence from obligations. Recusal is that kind of issue where judges' capabilities are tested on the basis of temperament. It is a tenet that no one should be judges in his or her own case. Courts must uphold their promises of providing fair and impartial justice by resolving controversies without bias. The practice of recusal, when and how an individual judge should be barred from adjudicating in a specific case in which he has an interest.

The opinions of the various scholars in India is that, "Several laws were passed by the parliament and state legislature, through this legislation various tribunals, commissions and other bodies were constituted where the persons who have been the judges of high Courts and Supreme Court of India were appointed. There are also non-statutory commissions like 'Law commission of India' where retired judges of high court and Supreme Court may be appointed".[9]The authors stated that, "The question arises here is that whether Central Government or State Government is bound to consult with Chief justice of SC and respective HC where the retired judges of that court going to appoint to a commission, tribunal or other similar body"?[10] Actually this question will arrive only where the concerned statute is silent relating to appointment or does not provide a specific mode of appointment.

The first 'Law Commission of India', headed by M. C. Setalvad, had briefly dealt with this issue. In paragraph 28 of the report, the Commission states: "we have noticed the only bar imposed on a Judge of the Supreme Court who has retired is that he shall not thereafter plead or act in any Court or before any authority. In the result, some Supreme Court Judges have, after retirement, set up chamber practice while some others have found employment in important positions under the Government. We have grave doubts whether starting chamber practice after retirement is consistent with the dignity of these retired judges and consonant with the high traditions which retired judges observe in other countries."[11]

"Where is appointment a retired High Court judge to a tribunal or commission lies within the discretion of the Central government or state government and if the consultation with Chief justice of the Supreme Court or the High Court is not approved then there is chances that government will make bias and favourable decision in related to appointment of judges which would indirectly affect the independence and integrity of judicial system. There may be chances come across where appointment have been made on selfishness other than merit and concentrate on political consideration".[12]To dilute the scope for any such inappropriate considerations there should be appropriate law where retired judged will be appointed to a commission or tribunal only with the consultation of Chief justice of concerned court. It means that Consultation with the Chief Justice of the Supreme Court and High Court would be mandatory.

Development in Indian Judiciary

The Supreme Court in *State of A.P.* v. *K. Mohanlal*[13], issue of this case was that "appointment of judicial and revenue members to the Special Court constituted under section 7 of the A.P. Land-grabbing (Prohibition) Act, 1982". In this case, "The state legislation provided that the chairman of the Special Court shall be appointed after consultation with the High Court Chief Justice and in case of the nomination by the respective HC for appointment then consensus with the chief Justice of SC if necessary (in case of the sitting judge of the High Court). In this case no consultation process was applied in appointment judicial members and revenue members".[14]

"A contention was raised before the Supreme Court that appointment of members of the tribunal without consulting the chief justice of the High Court concerned, Act shall be declared unconstitutional."[15]The Supreme Court rejected the contention raised and upheld the validity of the Act. This decision is related to the 'consultation' process but it was related to validity of the state legislation. "The decision, it must be remembered, was concerned only with the constitutional validity of enactment and not with the desirability of such consultation".[16]

So, in the provision of appointment of retired judges in commission or tribunal as a judge then consultation with Chief justice of Supreme Court and High Court has to be mandatory.

Anangav Udaya Singh Deo v. *Ranganath Misra*[17], In this case, "the issue before the High Court was whether the respondent, a former Chief Justice of India, could become a Member of Parliament of Rajya Sabha in light of the restriction in Article 124(7) of the Constitution. Repelling the contention that Parliament was an 'authority' and becoming a Member of Parliament would constitute 'acting' for purposes of the said article, the Court held that in interpreting Article 124(7), attention must be paid to Article 220, the analogous provision for High Court judges, specifically to its marginal note which read: "Restriction on practice after being a permanent judge." Accordingly, the restriction in Article 124(7) should be limited to post-retirement practice. Since acting as a legislator did not constitute such practice, the bar would not apply".[18]

Recent issue

"Justice Gogoi has nominated to Rajya Sabha and the appointment of Justice Sathasivam as a Governor". In these cases a lot of public criticism aroused against the judicial system and judicial independence, many of the legal scholars opined that this appointment is based on pure political desire and favoritism. The citizens are losing faith and the independence of judiciary which is a serious threat for democracy and justice delivery system, even Dr. B. R. Ambedkar has cautioned that once judiciary be corrupted, it will evil day for democracy.

JUDICIAL RECUSAL

A judge may sometimes meet in a situation where differences of interest arise or apparent conflict of interest requires him to recuse from the case. On the ground of bias, the recusal of judges is required. While on the ground of bias, a judge may have to evaluate not only on the basis of real likelihood of bias but also on the ground of reasonable suspicion of bias.

RECUSAL OF JUDGES IN INDIA

It is the practice in the Supreme Court of India and HC'S judges may not sit on the issue which is connected with his respective state and accumulate the dispute is a very serious. In India there, is absence of any legislation on recusal; several commissions and conferences have discussed the issue and laid down some of the principles.

In India, there is no statute laying down the minimum procedure which judges must follow in order to ensure impartiality.

RECENT CASES

- ***Central Bureau of Investigation case*[19]:**

In this case of Mr. Nageshwara Rao was appointed as chief of the CBI instead of the AlokVerma was removed by the government of India.

This appointment of Mr. Nageshwara Rao was challenged before SC of India where judges were recused themselves to hear the matter, the names of the judges were Chief Justice Ranjan Gagoi, Justice Ramana and Justice A.k. Sikri. "Rao was continued to be a director after former CBI director AlokVerma was removed by the high-power selection panel headed by PM Modi".[20]

It has been reported by one of the newspaper that, "The plea by non-government organization (NGO) Common Cause sought the quashing of the order of 10 January and argued that Rao's appointment as interim director was not according to the constitutional principles and principles in high power appointment usually done in selection considered to be illegal, arbitrary, mala fide and in infringement of the provisions of the Delhi Special Police Establishment Act (DSPE Act)".[21]

"Appointment of Mr. Rao as a CBI director was considered unauthenticated and legal. It seems that committee has been neglected by the Centre which was acting without jurisdiction appointed Rao,"[22] the plea was added.

***Ayodhya case*[23]:**

In this case, lawyer for the Sunni Central Waqf Board, senior advocate Rajeev Dhavan pointed out that Justice Uday Lalit had appeared as counsel in the Kalyan Singh case related to the Babri Masjid-Ram Janmabhoomi structure demolition. Kalyan Sing was the Chief Minister at that time when Babri Mazid was robbed by the people. Senior advocate Harish Salve spoke up for the judge, saying that it was a different case. The Kalyan Singh case appeared in 1997. It was the judge's discretion to recuse the case.

Bhima Koregaon case[24]:

Justice B.R. Gavai voluntarily left the case which was related Bhima Koregaon riots. The petition was filed by Navlakha for bail application against the decision of "Bombay High Court refused to quash the FIR registered against him by Pune police" under the provisions of the "Unlawful Activities Prevention Act and the Indian Penal Code. Appeal filed by the Navlakha came before a bench consist of justices NV Ramana, R Subhash Reddy and BR Gavai".[25]

In this case also, CJI Gogoi also refused to hear the petition and not cited any reason for the recusal. "Bombay High Court Judges including Justice Ranjit More and Dongre refused to cancel the FIR filed against Navlakha because there is prima facie material available against him which contain documents where Novlakha in work against the violence during Bhima Koregaon appeared in 2018".[26]

Recusal cases in 2021-22

Table 1.9

Case	Judges	Date
River Krishna Water Dispute case	Justice Chandrachud and Justice A. S. Boppanna	3 January 2022
Post poll violence case against Mamata Banerjee	Justice Anirudhha Bose &Justice Indira Banerjee	June 2021

The principle of judicial independence is intended to safeguard the justice system and the rule of law. To maintain public trust and confidence in the court, it is imperative that in the present legal system, some critical components of our judicial mechanism need to be revised.

Unless there are reasonable grounds for recusal, a constitutionally appointed judge is obliged to sit on any case assigned to them. The judges should recuse themselves if there is an apprehension that they might bring an impartial mind to the settlement of the question which judges have to decide. Instead of probability, the principle for recusal is a real and not remote possibility.

The analysis is divided into two stages. The judge should always consider first what reasonably leads to apprehension by a fully informed observer that the judge might decide the case other than on its merit; and secondly, whether there is a logical and sufficient connection between those circumstances and that apprehension.

In India there is no guidelines on what basis judges shall recuse themselves from the case. So, it hurt the judicial process and the right of the litigants.

Conclusion:

- "Ideally, the retired judges should reject such sinecures in the collective interest of the institution that they have served for many years. It is also a trend that people do not hesitate to link pre-retirement judgments of judges to their post-retirement conduct to secure lucrative appointments. This is an extremely dangerous perception for the institution of the judiciary. It badly tarnishes the image of the judicial system. The time has come when all the stakeholders of the legal profession should sit together to find out a long-lasting solution of this problem."
- Judges shall not accept any posts after retirements if the rule of law or independence of the judiciary will be on stake.
- Age of the Retirements of the SC and HC judges shall be increased so, then issues of post-retirements benefits to judges will not arrive.
- For inevitable appointments of post retirement recruitment a high level committee or commission of SC and HC judges has to be created.
- Article 124 and 217 shall be amended if post retirement jobs of the SC and HC judges want to be continued, in this way it may be controlled by proper law.
- Judges will perform their duties and exercise powers as judge honourably, faithfully, impartially and conscientiously."
- Edible equilibrium between judge's self-autonomy and judicial accountability.

- A judge has a constitutional duty when despairing justice and rendering judgements fairly while presiding once a case. When judges are assigned to a case, they should review the facts of the case impartially and determine whether they have any conflict of interest that would possibly prevent them from being impartial, ethical and fair.
- There is no statute in India that specifies the minimum procedure that judges must follow to ensure impartiality. However, courts have always insisted that judges and other adjudicatory authorities must adhere to impartiality principles. The principles of natural justice have evolved alongside the progress of civilization.
- A law for recusal shall be passed by the Parliament of India.
- Judges shall provide the reason of the recusal in every case.

References

[1]*Id.*
[2]Kharel Rajendra, "Recusal and Disqualification of Judges: An Overview"4 *NJA Law Journal* 13-24 (2010).
[3]*Id.*
[4]Kharel Rajendra, "Recusal and Disqualification of Judges: An Overview"4 *NJA Law Journal* 13-24 (2010).
[5]*Id.*
[6]ManeeshChhibber, "Recusal has become a selective call of morality for Supreme Court judges," 2019 *available at*: https://theprint.in/opinion/recusal-supreme-court-judges-gautam-navlakha-kashmir-cji-gogoi/303036/.
[7]*Ram Jawayav. State of Punjab* AIR 1955 SC 549.
[8]*Id.*
[9]Priyadarshini Barua, Sarthak Makkar and Vasanthi Hariharan, "Judicial Recusal: A Comparative Analysis Editorial" 7 *GNLU Law Review* 1–16 (2020).
[10]Kharel Rajendra, "Recusal and Disqualification of Judges: An Overview"4 *NJA Law Journal* 13-24 (2010).

[11]Lokendra Malik, "Chapter 5 Post-Retirement Assignments of the Supreme Court Judges in India: A Critical Analysis" *SSRN Electronic Journal* 39 (2020).
[12]*Id.*
[13]*State of A.P.* v. *K. Mohanlal* (1998) 5 SCC 468.
[14]*Id.*
[15]*Id.*
[16]*Id.*
[17] AIR 2000 Ori 24.
[18]Lokendra Malik, "Chapter 5 Post-Retirement Assignments of the Supreme Court Judges in India: A Critical Analysis" *SSRN Electronic Journal* 39 (2020).
[19]"Supreme Court holds CBI's ex-interim chief Nageswara Rao guilty of contempt", *The Hindu*, 12-2-2019, *available at* https://www.livemint.com/politics/news/another-judge-recuses-himself-from-hearing-plea-against-cbi-s-rao-1548914117000.html; (last visited September 10, 2020).
[20]*Id.*
[21]*Id.*
[22]*Id.*
[23]*M Siddiq (D) ThrLrs* v. *Mahant Suresh Das &Ors.*(decided by SC in November 9, 1919).
[24]Bhima Koregaon case: Another Supreme Court Judge recuses himself from hearing Gautam Navlakha's plea, *The Leaflet*, 1/10/2019, *available at* https://www.theleaflet.in/bhima-koregaon-case-another-supreme-court-judge-recuses-himself-from-hearing-gautam-navlakhas-plea/#; (last visited on 10 September 2020).
[25]*Id.*
[26]*Id.*

Publisher: Eliva Press Global Ltd

Email: info@elivapress.com

Made in United States
Orlando, FL
04 November 2026

90219744R00115